Scorn

Inca-Kola
So Far So Good
Look Behind You

Scorn

A bucketful of discourtesy, disparagement, invective,
ridicule, impudence, contumely, derision, hate, affront,
disdain, bile, taunts, curses and jibes

EDITED BY MATTHEW PARRIS

ASSISTANT EDITORS:
DAVID PROSSER AND SIMON CHRISTMAS

HAMISH HAMILTON · LONDON

HAMISH HAMILTON LTD

Published by the Penguin Group
Penguin Books Ltd, 27 Wrights Lane, London W8 5TZ, England
Penguin Books USA Inc., 375 Hudson Street, New York, New York 10014, USA
Penguin Books Australia Ltd, Ringwood, Victoria, Australia
Penguin Books Canada Ltd, 10 Alcorn Avenue, Toronto, Ontario, Canada M4V 3B2
Penguin Books (NZ) Ltd, 182–190 Wairau Road, Auckland 10, New Zealand

Penguin Books Ltd, Registered Offices: Harmondsworth, Middlesex, England

First published 1994
1 3 5 7 9 10 8 6 4 2

Filmset in 10/11.5pt Bembo by Selwood Systems, Midsomer Norton

Printed in Great Britain by Butler & Tanner Ltd, Frome and London

A CIP catalogue record for this book is available from the British Library

ISBN 0–241–13384–X

To Lady Thatcher, who gave me my first job in politics, who caused me to be elected to Parliament, the mockery of whom furnished me for five years with the staple of my trade as sketchwriter, who forms the object of the largest single and sustained body of scorn in what follows, who rises above it all, and who, if her permission for this dedication had been sought, would undoubtedly have refused it.

Introduction

This is not a textbook. I have not strung out the entries in a dry, chronological list. Nor have I attempted to divide them into neat sections – 'attacks on honour', 'attacks on appearance', 'attacks on ability', etc. – or where would you put the remark that a man's an incompetent, warty scoundrel? Instead, I have tried to order these quotations in a way that allows them to speak, one to another.

Scanning my chosen remarks, many struck me as voices answering, echoing or rebuking each other down the ages. Often there seemed to be a dialogue going on, sometimes between people who had never heard of each other, sometimes between people who had. So I have tried to arrange my quotations as a sort of conversation, a 'volley'. Often – not always – this works well. Sometimes the thread linking the dialogue is tenuous. Occasionally it may break. Volleys are not continuous. More than once a new voice will take the ball and run with it to a different court. But the feelings and ideas which link human expressions of scorn have enough in common to bounce these quotations off each other in a verbal sport which, at least sometimes, finds meaning and momentum.

The direction of the conversation has been signposted, by topic, very broadly in the headings at the top of each page. Those seeking quotations on a particular theme will find these signposts listed in the Contents and there is an index of authors and victims at the end. But I hope that this dialogue of voices has enough shape to invite its being read as a play, rather than consulted as a directory.

A play or directory of what? There are many excellent anthologies of insult, which I have consulted freely, some of which are credited in the Acknowledgements. But they leave so much out. 'Insult' is too restrictive. '*Scorn*' became my chosen title, for language can be used to express anger, hatred or disapprobation in a range of ways of which simple insult is only a part. When Job curses the day he was conceived, he scorns life itself, but this is not really an insult. When Hobbes describes human society as 'nasty, brutish, and short', that is scorn, not insult. Neither is 'witty'. Neither are 'put-downs'. Wit and put-down – taking a verbal dig at others – are a part of scorn, but not the whole of it. What I have tried to explore has been the dark side of language: humorous or serious, the use of the spoken and written word to hurt, wound or ridicule – to decry not just other persons but things too: and art, and life, and God himself.

The language of scorn, though vast, finds itself pursuing one or more of only four purposes. The first purpose is part factual, part polemical: the *indictment* – the conveying of hurtful facts or a hurtful argument; the use of words to prosecute or defame. The literature is enormous and a little outside my theme; it finds a handful of examples in this book, such as Burke's indictment of Warren Hastings.

The second is not to persuade or inform but to discomfort by a reference to existing, agreed knowledge: *mockery* – words which allude to something already known or suspected but whose mention, precisely because it is known, is hurtful. It could be, for example, a reference to someone's big nose or humble parentage, or a physical or moral defect, a failing.

A third purpose of scorn comprises the very simplest form of abuse: the nose-thumb or *snarl*. This is the use of language in circumstances where the alternative might be to spit, an expression of pure hatred: 'I loathe you' or 'yah-boo-sucks'. Such abuse conveys neither reason nor justification for the scorn; it conveys the scorn alone.

And finally the most curious of the four: the *curse* – a verbal formula used to invoke some malign external power to hurt one's victim. This uses words as we might use a pin to stick in a voodoo doll.

It is fascinating to observe the decline in the potency and frequency of real cursing between ancient times and our own. God and the prophets do a great deal of it in the Old (and to some extent the New) Testament. Judaism and Islam use the curse. So did the ancient Egyptians – we include here Tutankhamun's curse. In early times, in primitive cultures now, and very strongly in Eastern European cultures today, the use of language to curse is rich and lively, while the use of wit, indictment and other verbal abuse is often disappointingly crude.

As faith in the supernatural declines, so does the living curse. It degenerates into a notional curse ('damn you', 'a plague on both your houses') which neither alludes to any actual failing nor conveys real information. It takes the form of a curse but is not a true curse: it is just a snarl. Modern cursing, though common, is uninteresting and routine because its soul is dead. We have lost our link with the supernatural. Correspondingly, other forms of scorn have been getting cleverer and wittier since the ancients. Words, stripped of the innate magical powers invoked by the simple act of pronouncing them, are obliged to carry interest and meaning in their own right.

As I gathered material for this book, it became clear that the curse is really a subject on its own, and needs an anthology of its own; it cannot be properly integrated into other forms of verbal abuse. But it is too interesting to ignore. I have therefore included a short, first section in which a sampler of curses, from ancient to modern times, is assembled more as a list than a dialogue.

Scorn has not been difficult to collect. The British Library, the Cambridge University library, and appeals for suggestions to some 500 people in public or academic life have brought in a wealth of material. The problem, as ever, has been what to leave out. For a short book one must leave out most. This collection is therefore utterly and unapologetically idiosyncratic. It most emphatically is an anthology and not a dictionary, and I have included or excluded arbitrarily and at whim. Many, many famous quips are missing because they are already very well known, and available in a score of insult collections or dictionaries of quotations. Churchill and Dorothy Parker are here only occasionally.

I have had a problem with Shakespeare. His work alone yields a treasury of insult, and such a collection has already been published. But, though he provides both wit and argument in his scorning, Shakespeare is really outstanding for his simple, schoolboyish, but verbally dazzling *mockery*. A glance at his vocabulary of insult gives the impression of relentless verbal heavy-shelling of a gloriously crude kind: 'Thou drone, thou snail, thou slug, thou sot', 'breath of garlic-eaters!', 'you mad mustachio purple-hued maltworms!', 'leathern-jerkin, crystal-button, not-pated, agate-ring, puke-stocking, caddis-garter, smooth-tongue, Spanish pouch!', 'Whoreson, obscene, greasy tallow-catch', 'oh polished perturbation!', 'you Banbury cheese!', 'show your sheep-biting face', 'stale old mouse-eaten dry cheese', 'I will smite his noddles!', 'you whoreson upright rabbit!', 'you fustilarian! I'll tickle your catastrophe!'. You could fill a book with this; I have decided to let others do so. Fascinating – to me – has been what, in Shakespeare's case, the insults reveal about the insulter. Scorn tells us much – unwittingly – about the tastes and prejudices of the scorner. Shakespeare's real horror was of grossness. He hated urine, foul odours and uncleanness. Unlike many others, he rarely attacks women, but can be coldly, horribly dismissive of them. I have become convinced that Shakespeare was a fastidious gay man.

Scorn also reveals much about the offensive–defensive divide. Its literature is crammed full – starting spectacularly with the Romans – of anti-homosexual invective, the key image being that of the effeminate, passive gay man who is buggered by others. Only very recently, however, do we begin to find confident answering invective from the gay camp (or camp gay?). There is much anti-Semitic insult, less insult returned. Anti-black invective is prodigious and rich; anti-white invective is edgy, defensive and scarce.

Finally, attribution has often been a problem. A handful of individuals in political and literary history – Dr Johnson, Disraeli, Churchill, Dorothy Parker, for instance – have become so famous for their wit and scorn that the world has begun to attribute to them sayings which more careful research reveals were not theirs. Further, famous scorners begin to attract their Boswells, and find their conversation recorded and remembered, where ours would be forgotten, or unattributed. It seems that if you acquire a sufficiently powerful reputation for insult, the reputation will begin to grow by its own momentum, as everything you say is noted, and extra sayings of unknown authorship are attributed, speculatively, to you!

Gathering this collection has been fun. But more than a year of staring at unremitting lists of unpleasant remarks does, eventually, lower the spirits. I am looking forward to raising my eyes at last from the bucketful of misery and spite which follows.

MATTHEW PARRIS
Derbyshire, June 1994

Acknowledgements

Nothing in this book is new. To my two assistant editors, David Prosser and Simon Christmas, has fallen the task of gathering the mountain from which I have assembled this personal molehill of an anthology. They have worked hard for two years, and I am grateful. I have relied not only on their industry, but on their judgement. David managed the project.

My thanks to those hundreds of friends and long-shot acquaintances whom we contacted for suggestions, many of which have found their way into the book. Thanks too to Dr Richard Parkinson at the British Museum and to the editors of dozens of dictionaries, anthologies and works of reference in this field, on whose research we have drawn. These are too numerous to list in full, but the following have been particularly useful:

An Anthology of Invective and Abuse, ed. Hugh Kingsmill (London, 1930); *A Dictionary of Contemporary Quotations*, ed. Jonathon Green (London, 1982); *A Dictionary of International Slurs*, ed. A. A. Roback (Wisconsin, 1979); *A Dictionary of Sexist Quotations*, ed. Selma James (Hemel Hempstead, 1984); *The Garden of Priapus: Sexuality and Aggression in Roman Humour* by Amy Richlin (London, 1983); *The Guinness Dictionary of Poisonous Quotes*, ed. Colin Jarman (London, 1991); *Lexicon of Musical Invective* by Nicholas Slonimsky (Washington, DC, 1965); *Maledicta: the International Journal of Verbal Aggression*, ed. Rheinhold Aman (1977–86); *Picking on Men* by Judy Allen (London, 1985); *Shakespeare's Insults*, ed.

Acknowledgements

Wayne Hill and Cynthia J. Ottchen (Cambridge, 1992).

Acknowledgement is also due to HarperCollins Publishers Limited and Germaine Greer for *The Female Eunuch*; to William Heinemann Ltd for *Cakes and Ale* by W. Somerset Maugham; to Guy Lee for *The Poems of Catullus* (OUP, 1990) by permission of Oxford University Press; to The Society of Authors on behalf of the Bernard Shaw Estate; to John Murray (Publishers) Ltd for *Slough* by John Betjeman; to Laurence Pollinger Ltd and the Estate of Frieda Lawrence Ravagli for *How Beastly the Bourgeois Is* by D. H. Lawrence; to David Higham Associates and Osbert Sitwell for *A Certain Statesman*; to Channel 4 and Open Media Limited for the Dennis Potter; and to Faber and Faber Ltd for the following extracts: Philip Larkin's 'This be the Verse' from *High Windows*; W. H. Auden's *Six Odes IV* (*To John Warner, Son of Rex and Frances Warner*); and John Osborne's *Look Back in Anger*.

The illustration on page 1 is reprinted courtesy of the British Museum Department of Egyptian Antiquities.

Every effort has been made to trace copyright holders. The publishers apologize for any errors or omissions, and would be grateful to be notified of any corrections that should appear in any reprint.

My dear secretary, Eileen Wright, has laboured, to draw together the strings of my disjointed endeavours. To her, as ever, thanks.

Come 'ere, you fucker.

This, the earliest recorded insult I have found, dates from around 2300 BC. It is from the tomb of Ti at Saqqara, Egypt. The hieroglyph (circled) is fairly self-explanatory. Academics have rendered the insult, which one fisherman is hurling at another, as 'Come here, you copulator'

His heart shall not be content in life, he shall receive no water in the necropolis and his soul shall be destroyed for eternity.

Egyptian curse, inscription aimed at 'anyone who desecrates the tomb-chapel'

May you get fucked by a donkey! May your wife get fucked by a donkey! May your child fuck your wife!

Egyptian legal curse, c. 950 BC

After this opened Job his mouth, and cursed his day. And Job spake, and said, Let the day perish wherein I was born, and the night *in which* it was said, There is a man child conceived. Let that day be darkness; let not God regard it from above, neither let the light shine upon it; ... let the blackness of the day terrify it. *As for* that night, let darkness seize upon it; let it not be joined unto the days of the year, let it not come into the number of the months. Lo, let that night be solitary, let no joyful voice come therein. Let them curse it that curse the day, who are ready to raise up their mourning. Let the stars of the twilight thereof be dark; let it look for light, but *have* none; neither let it see the dawning of the day: Because it shut not up the doors of my *mother's* womb, nor hid sorrow from mine eyes. Why died I not from the womb? *why* did I *not* give up the ghost when I came out of the belly? Why did the knees prevent me? or why the breasts that I should suck? ... Wherefore is light given to him that is in misery, and life unto the bitter *in* soul; Which long for death, but it *cometh* not; and dig for it more than for hid treasures; Which rejoice exceedingly, *and* are glad, when they can find the grave?

Job cursing the day he was born, Job 3: 1–22

Cursed *shalt* thou *be* in the city, and cursed *shalt* thou *be* in the field.

Cursed *shall be* thy basket and thy store.

Cursed *shall be* the fruit of thy body, and the fruit of thy land, the increase of thy kine, and the flocks of thy sheep.

Cursed *shalt* thou *be* when thou comest in, and cursed *shalt* thou *be* when thou goest out . . .

Moses' curse in Deuteronomy 28: 16–19

May the earth refuse thee her fruits and the river his waters, may wind and breeze deny their breath. May the sun not be warm for thee, nor Phoebe bright, may the clear stars fail thy vision. May neither Vulcan nor the air lend thee their aid, nor earth nor sea afford thee any path. Mayst thou wander an exile and destitute, and haunt the doors of others, and beg a little food with trembling mouth. May neither thy body nor thy sick mind be free from querulous pain, may night be to thee more grievous than day, and day than night. Mayst thou ever be piteous, but have none to pity thee; may men and women rejoice at thy adversity. May hatred crown thy tears, and mayst thou be thought worthy, having borne many ills, to bear yet more. And (what is rare) may the aspect of thy fortune, though its wonted favour be lost, bring thee but ill-will. Mayst thou have cause enough for death, but no means of dying; may thy life be compelled to shun the death it prays for. May thy spirit struggle long ere it leave thy tortured limbs, and rack thee first with long delaying.

Ovid, *Ibis*, tr. J. H. Mozley

But the Jews will not be pleased with thee, neither the Christians, until thou follow their religion; say, The Direction of God is the true direction. And verily if thou follow their desires, after the knowledge which hath been given thee, thou shalt find no patron or protector against God. They to whom we have given the book of the Koran, and who read it with its true reading, they believe therein; and whoever believeth not therein, they shall perish.

Koran, II

O pour out thy wrath upon the heathen who know thee not, and upon the kingdoms who invoke not thy name; for they have devoured Jacob and laid waste his beautiful dwelling. Pour out thy indignation upon them and cause thy fierce anger to overtake them. Pursue them in wrath and destroy them from under the heavens of the Lord.

Judaic curse ritually invoked at the Passover between the third and fourth cups of wine. The door to the outside must be opened for its pronouncement. Leo Abse, who referred the editor to this curse, said he had been told that, at times of danger, isolation and persecution, the pronouncement of this curse upon their persecutors was a source of great comfort to Jews assembled for the Passover

May you croak in the faith of the Poles!

Ukrainian, regarded as an outrageous curse

May the fleas of a thousand camels infest your armpits.

Arab curse

Careful: my knife drills your soul
listen,   [name victim]
One of the wolf people
listen   I'll grind your saliva into the earth
listen   I'll cover your bones with black flint

listen   I'll cover your bones with black feathers
listen   I'll cover your bones with black rocks
Because you're going where it's empty
Black coffin out on the hill
listen   the black earth will hide you, will
find you a black hut
Out where it's dark, in that country
listen   I'm bringing a box for your bones
A black box
A grave with black pebbles
listen   your soul's spilling out
listen   it's blue.

Cherokee Indian chant designed to bring about the death of a victim, adapted
by Jerome Rothenberg, *Sacred Formulas of the Cherokees*

May you dig up your Father by moonlight and make soup of
his bones.

Fiji Islands curse

Cursed be your mother's anus
   Cursed be your father's testicles.

Yoruba verbal duelling, quoted by Chief Oludare Olajuba, *References to Sex
in Yoruba Oral Literature*

Go in your Mother's cunt.

Serbian insult

Go to holy shit!

Cuban insult

I shit on the balls of your dead ones.

Spanish gypsy insult

Go to the prick's house!
Cuban insult

Copulate with my Father who is dead.
Admiralty Islands' most unpardonable insult

I shit in your Mother's milk.
Spanish insult

Copulate with your wife.
Trobriand Islands' most unpardonable insult

I hope that your piles hang like a bunch of grapes.
Greek insult directed at homosexuals

I shit on your Father's nose.
Farsi (Iranian) insult

I shit on God, on the cross, and on the carpenter who made it (and on the son of the whore who planted the pine)!
Catalan insult

May shit be on your hair.
Farsi (Iranian) insult for women

I shit on the cock of Passion!
Catalan insult

May a fart be on your beard
Farsi (Iranian) insult for men

Christ is a bastard . . . Christ is a whoremaster . . . God damn and confound all Gods.
John Taylor, fined and imprisoned for blasphemy in the eighteenth century

May the devil damn you to the stone of dirges, or to the well of ashes seven miles below hell; and may the devil break your bones! And all my calamity and harm and misfortune for a year on you!

Curse from the Cois Fharraige, west of Galway City, in Connemara

I will tear your crotch apart.

Farsi (Iranian) insult between women

I'll stick a pig's leg up your cunt until your back-teeth rattle.

Japanese insult

A donkey's head in your cunt.

Farsi (Iranian) insult used by a woman to call another stupid

May hound-wounding, heart-ache, and vultures gouging her
    eyes,
Derangement and madness on her mind come soon!
May the entrails and mansion of pleasure out of this worm
    fall out!
But may she still be alive till everyone's sick of the sight!

Peadar Ó Doirín, 'An Guairne'

A plague o' both your houses!

William Shakespeare, *Romeo and Juliet*

Woe unto bloody Lichfield!

George Fox, founder of the Quakers

You common cry of curs! whose breath I hate
As reek o' the rotten fens, whose loves I prize
As the dead carcases of unburied men
That do corrupt my air, I banish you;

Curses

And here remain with your uncertainty!
Let every feeble rumour shake your hearts!
Your enemies, with nodding of their plumes,
Fan you into despair! Have the power still
To banish your defenders; till at length
Your ignorance – which finds not till it feels,
Making but reservation of yourselves,
Still your own foes – deliver you as most
Abated captives to some nation
That won you without blows!
William Shakespeare, Coriolanus's farewell to his fellow-citizens, *Coriolanus*

Thou cursed cock, with thy perpetual noise,
May'st thou be capon made, and lose thy voice,
Or on a dunghill may'st thou spend thy blood,
And vermin prey upon thy craven brood;
May rivals tread thy hens before thy face
Then with redoubled courage give thee chase;
May'st thou be punished for St Peter's crime,
And on Shrove Tuesday perish in thy prime;
May thy bruised carcass be some beggar's feast –
Thou first and worst disturber of man's rest.
Sir Charles Sedley, 'On a cock at Rochester'

May you be cursed with chronic anxiety about the weather.
John Burroughs

I charm thy life
From the weapons of strife,
From stone and from wood,
From fire and from flood,

From the serpent's tooth,
And the beasts of blood:
From Sickness I charm thee,
And Time shall not harm thee;
But Earth which is mine,
Its fruits shall deny thee;
And Water shall hear me,
And know thee and fly thee;
And the Winds shall not touch thee
When they pass by thee,
And the Dews shall not wet thee,
When they fall nigh thee:
And thou shalt seek Death
To release thee, in vain;
Thou shalt live in thy pain
While Kehama shall reign,
With a fire in thy heart,
And a fire in thy brain;
And Sleep shall obey me,
And visit thee never,
And the Curse shall be on thee
For ever and ever.
Robert Southey, *The Curse of Kehama*

you are the dumbest thing
on the earth the slimiest
most rotten thing in the universe
you motherfuckin germ
you konk-haired blood suckin punks
you serpents of pestilence you

samboes you green witches gnawing the heads of infants
you rodents you whores
you sodomites you fat
slimy cockroaches crawling to your
holes with bits of malcolm's flesh
i hope you are smothered
in the fall of a huge yellow moon.

Welton Smith on black people who failed to support Malcolm X, *The Nigga Section*

Sadaam, oh Sadaam
Thou flesh-knotter you
Claim not to be Muslim
For you are truly a Jew
Your deeds have proved ugly
Your face is darkest black
And we will set fire
To your bottom and your back

Poem on Sadaam Hussein, broadcast on Saudi television during the Gulf War

Son of a Scots manse though you were
I've taken the rare scunner against you,
You who thieve the golden hours of bairns,
You who bitch up the world's peoples
With crystal images, pitch-black lies,
You who have ended civilized conversation
And dished out licences to print banknotes,
May your soul shrink to the size of a midge
And never rest in a couthie kirkyard
But dart across a million wee screens
And be harassed by TV jingles for ever and ever,

For thine's the kingdom of the *televisor*,
You goddam bloody genius, John Logie Baird!
Robert Greacen, 'Curse'

Fuck you.
Ed Koch, in response to a reporter's allegations of war criminality, and
countless others

I hope you will pray too that the Lord will smite him hip and
thigh, bone and marrow, heart and lungs and all there is to
him; that he shall destroy him quickly and utterly.
Bob Jones III, a Christian fundamentalist, on Alexander Haig, after the latter
refused Ian Paisley a visa to visit the USA

Fuck off, Norway.
Paul Gascoigne, when asked by live Norwegian television if he had a message
for the Norwegian people before the England–Norway World Cup qualifier

I fart in your general direction.
Monty Python and the Holy Grail

Now I can finally say what a diplomat normally cannot to
those he comes into contact with: I hope you encounter every
curse imaginable!
Koji Haneda, First Secretary, Embassy of Japan (London), closing a letter to
the editor of this book

We praise the man who is angry on the right grounds, against the right persons, in the right manner, at the right moment, and for the right length of time.
Aristotle, *Nicomachean Ethics*, IV

imanis metula es. [You're a big prick.]
Pompeii graffiti

Your arsehole is filled with blue mud.
South-east Salish (North American Indian) insult

commictae spurca saliva lupae. [The foul saliva of a pissed–over whore.]
Catullus, XCIX.10, tr. Amy Richlin

Your blistered crotch!
Insult from the Marquesas Islands

Lahis felat a.II. [Lahis gives blow jobs for $2.]
Pompeii graffiti

Your mouth and your arsehole smell the same, Theodorus,
So much so that it would be a good trick for doctors to tell
    them apart.
You should certainly have made a sign saying which was your
    mouth, which your arsehole.
Just now when you were gabbing, I thought you'd farted.
Nicharchus, from the Greek

Cosmus Equitiaes magnus cinaedus et fellator est suris apertis. [Equitias' slave Cosmus is a big queer and a cocksucker with his legs wide open.]
Pompeii graffiti

I thought (so help me Gods!) it made no difference
  Whether I smelt Aemilius' mouth or arsehole,
One being no cleaner, the other no filthier.
  But in fact the arsehole's cleaner and kinder:
It has no teeth. The mouth has teeth half a yard long
  And gums like an ancient wagon-chassis.
Moreover, when it opens up it's like the cunt
  Of a pissing mule gaping in a heat wave.

Catullus, xcvii, tr. Guy Lee

Zoile, quid solium subluto podice perdis?
Spurcius ut fiat, Zoile, merge caput.
[Zoilus, if you want to pollute the public bathing place,
Don't stick in your ass first, stick in your face.]

Martial, ii.42, tr. Richard O'Connell

Vibennius and son – believed
The public baths' best pair of thieves.
(Father's filthy hands go roving
Through some hapless bather's clothing
Whilst, elsewhere, the son has got 'em
Wedged up his voracious bottom.)
Why don't you both just go to hell!
For Father's crimes are known too well,
And few among the punters crave
A boy whose buttocks need a shave.

Catullus, xxxiii, tr. Simon Christmas

If you were as narrow-arsed as you are narrow-minded, or
broad-minded as your anus is broad, you would be the most
perfect of people walking the earth.

Di'bil, from the Arabic

Sabina felas, no belle faces. [Sabina, you give blow-jobs, you don't do good.]

Pompeii graffiti. The original Latin, as in many of these examples from Pompeii, is misspelt. Amy Richlin has suggested this freestyle translation.

I am the Roman Emperor, and am above grammar.

Sigismund, when his Latin was criticized

You assumed the 'toga virilis', which you at once turned into a woman's toga. First you were a public whore, and the price of your shame was fixed, nor was it small; but soon Curio intervened, who led you away from the prostitution business and, as if he had given you your bridal gown, established you in a steady and fixed marriage. No boy bought for the sake of lust was ever so much in the power of his master as you were in Curio's. How many times his father threw you out of his own house, how many times he posted guards to keep you from crossing the threshold! But you, with night as your ally, your lust urging you on, and your payment compelling you, were let down through the roof-tiles. These shames that house could bear no longer. Don't you know I'm talking about things well known to me? Recall that time, when Curio the father was grieving, lying in bed, and his son flinging himself at my feet weeping entrusted you to me ... He himself, moreover, burning with love, affirmed that he could not bear the longing caused by your separation and would go into exile ... But now let us pass over your sex crimes and shameful acts; there are certain things which I cannot pronounce with decency; you, however, are that much freer, since you have allowed things to your discredit which

you could not hear named by an enemy who had any sense
of shame.
Cicero on Anthony, *Philippics*, 11.44–7, tr. Amy Richlin

Your stinking foreskin filth.
Polynesian insult

When you rise up from a chair, Lesbia,
(I've seen it happen frequently)
You get butt-fucked by your skirt.
The damned thing catches in the narrow crack
Between those massive buns of yours,
Those ship-crunching pillars of Hercules.
You pull with your left hand, you pull with your right,
Wincing and grunting till it comes loose.
An unladylike *faux pas*, to say the least.
Want a tip on etiquette, Lesbia?
Don't get up, and don't sit down.
Martial, xi.99, tr. Joseph Salemi

He waddles like an Armenian bride.
Osmanli insult

A waste of skin.
Lancashire expression

Their teeth, because of their foul food, are like the nails of a
female circumciser whose knives are too blunt.
Hassan Ibn Thabit, a contemporary of Muhammad, on the Hawazin

As flash as a rat with a gold tooth.
Australian expression

Villainous and loathsome screamer! Your audacity
fills the whole earth, the whole Assembly,
all taxes, all indictments, all law-courts,
you mud-churner, you who have thrown
our whole city into chaos and confusion,
you who have defeated our Athens with your shouting,
watching like the tunny-fishers from the rocks above for shoals
   of tribute.

Aristophanes on the Athenian general Cleon, *The Knights*. The words are
spoken by the chorus. Tr. Alan H. Sommerstein

The language of Aristophanes reeks of his miserable quackery:
it is made up of the lowest and most miserable puns; he doesn't
even please the people, and to men of judgement and honour
he is intolerable; his arrogance is insufferable, and all honest
men detest his malice.

Plutarch on Aristophanes

You're happy to get fucked, Saufeia,
But not to share a bath with me.
That something's very wrong is clear;
But not so clear what it might be.
Perhaps you know that from your chest
There hangs a pair of scraggy tits,
Or worry that, when you're undressed,
You've stretch marks round your nether bits.
Perhaps your groin is torn and mangled,
Gaping wide from back to front.
Perhaps an unknown something dangles
Tongue-like from your fleshy cunt.
But not at all, quite the reverse –

There's nothing wrong with what you've got.
The truth is that your fault is worse.
The truth is: you're an idiot.
Martial, III.72, tr. Simon Christmas

The classics are only primitive literature. They belong in the same class as primitive machinery and primitive music and primitive medicine.
Stephen Leacock, 'Homer and Humbug'

Plato is a bore.
Friedrich Nietzsche

The more I read him, the less I wonder that they poisoned him.
Thomas Babington Macaulay on Socrates

A crawling and disgusting parasite, a base scoundrel, and pander to unnatural passions.
William Cobbett on Virgil

Every man with a belly full of the classics is an enemy of the human race.
Henry Miller

A gentleman need not know Latin, but he should at least have forgotten it.
Brander Matthews. Attrib.

Then their itch can't bear delay, then woman acts her true
    self,
and from all equally the shout is repeated from the whole
    apse,
'Now it's right, let in the men.' The adulterer is asleep,

she orders a boy to grab his cloak and hurry over;
if there is none, she runs to the slaves; if you take away the
  hope
of slaves, the milkman comes, for a fee; if he
is sought and there are no men, there's no delay, for her part,
in putting her butt under a donkey.

Juvenal on women, VI.327–34, tr. Amy Richlin

'O Grandson of Conn, O Cormac,' said Carbre, 'how do you
  distinguish women?'
'Not hard to tell,' said Cormac. 'I distinguish them, but I
  make no difference among them.'

They are crabbed as constant companions
haughty when visited,
lewd when neglected . . .
stubborn in a quarrel,
not to be trusted with a secret . . .
boisterous in their jealousy . . .
lustful in bed . . .
Better to whip than to humour them . . .
better to scourge than to gladden them . . .
They are waves that drown you,
they are fires that burn you . . .
they are moths for sticking to one,
they are serpents for cunning . . .

The Instructions of King Cormac MacAirt

The male is by nature superior, and the female inferior: the
one rules and the other is ruled.

Aristotle, *Politics*, I.5

A good part – and definitely the most fun part – of being a feminist is about frightening men ... Of course, there's a lot more to feminism ... but scaring the shit out of the scumbags is an amusing and necessary part because, sadly, a good many men still respect nothing but strength.

Julie Burchill, in *Time Out*

Nature intended women to be our slaves ... they are our property; we are not theirs. They belong to us, just as a tree that bears fruit belongs to a gardener. What a mad idea to demand equality for women! ... Women are nothing but machines for producing children.

Napoleon Bonaparte

The male function is to produce sperm. We now have sperm banks.

Valerie Solanas, in *S. C. U. M. Manifesto*

Women who can, do. Those who cannot, become feminists.

Anonymous

I myself have never been able to find out precisely what feminism is: I only know that people call me a feminist whenever I express sentiments that differentiate me from a doormat.

Rebecca West

I consider that women who are authors, lawyers and politicians are monsters.

Auguste Renoir

When a woman inclines to learning there is usually something wrong with her sex apparatus.

Friedrich Nietzsche

I would venture to guess that Anon, who wrote so many poems without signing them, was often a woman.
Virginia Woolf, *A Room of One's Own*

A very little wit is valued in a woman; as we are pleased with a few words spoken plain by a parrot.
Jonathan Swift, *Thoughts on Various Subjects*

Sir, a woman's preaching is like a dog's walking upon his hind legs. It is not done well; but you are surprised to find it done at all.
Samuel Johnson

It is clearly absurd that it should be possible for a woman to qualify as a saint with direct access to the Almighty while she may not qualify as a curate.
Baroness Mary Stocks

We have no desire to say anything that might tend to encourage women to embark on accountancy, for although women might make excellent book-keepers, there is much in accountancy proper that is, we think, unsuitable for them.
English Institute of Chartered Accountants, in the *Accountant* (1912)

Woman was God's *second* mistake.
Friedrich Nietzsche

When God made man, she was only testing.
Graffiti in ladies' lavatory, London W11

All women are little balls of fluff in the eyes of the Creator.
Donald Pomerleau, Baltimore Police Commissioner, testifying in a sex discrimination case

Do you know why God withheld the sense of humour from women? That we may love you instead of laugh at you.
Mrs Patrick Campbell, to a man

A man is in general better pleased when he has a good dinner upon his table, than when his wife talks Greek.
Samuel Johnson

These are rare attainments for a damsel, but pray tell me, can she spin?
James I, when introduced to a young girl proficient in Latin, Greek and Hebrew. Attrib.

That woman can speak eighteen languages and she can't say 'no' in one of them.
Dorothy Parker of a guest surrounded by men at one of her parties

One tongue is sufficient for a woman.
John Milton, when asked if he would allow his daughters to learn foreign languages. Attrib.

As men
Do walk a mile, women should talk an hour,
After supper. 'Tis their exercise.
Francis Beaumont

Beneath this stone, a lump of clay
Lies Arabella Young
Who on the 21st of May
Began to hold her tongue.
Epitaph, Hatfield, Massachusetts

It has been said in the praise of some men, that they could talk whole hours together upon anything; but it must be owned to the honour of the other sex, that there are many among them who can talk whole hours together upon nothing ... I have often been puzzled to assign a cause why women should have this talent of ready utterance in so much greater perfection than men. I have sometime fancied that they have not a retentive power, or the faculty of suppressing their thoughts, as men have, but that they are necessitated to speak every thing they think ... A friend of mine, who is an excellent anatomist, had promised me by the first opportunity to dissect a women's tongue, and to examine whether there may not be in it certain juices which render it so wonderfully voluble or flippant, or whether the fibres of it may not be made up of a finer or more pliant thread; or whether there are not in it some particular muscles which dart it up and down by such sudden glances and vibrations; or whether, in the last place, there may not be certain undiscovered channels running from the head and the heart to this little instrument of loquacity, and conveying into it a perpetual affluency of animal spirits.

Joseph Addison, in the *Spectator*, 1711

Their [men's] slanderous tongues are so short, and the time wherein they have lavished out their words freely hath been so long, that they know we cannot catch hold of them to pull them out, and they think we will not write to reprove their lying lips.

Jane Anger, *Her Protection for Women*, 1589

To what purpose is it for women to make vows, when men have so many millions of ways to make them break them? And when sweet words, fair promises, tempting, flattering, swearing, lying will not serve to beguile the poor soul, then with rough handling, violence and plain strength of arms they are, or have been heretofore, rather made prisoners to lust's thieves than wives and companions to faithful honest lovers.

The Law's Resolutions of Women's Rights, published 1632 but probably written in the 1580s

All men are rapists and that's all they are. They rape us with their eyes, their laws and their cocks.

Marilyn French

A preface.
To all Women in general,
and gentle Reader whatsoever

Fie on the falsehood of men, whose minds go oft a-madding and whose tongues cannot so soon be wagging, but straight they fall a-tattling! Was there ever any so abused, so slandered, so railed upon, or so wickedly handled undeservedly, as are we women?

Jane Anger, *Her Protection for Women*, 1589

Most Women have no Characters at all.

Alexander Pope, *Epistles to Several Persons*, 'To a Lady'

Woman the fountain of all human frailty!
What mighty ills have not been done by woman?
Who was't betrayed the Capitol? A woman.
Who lost Mark Anthony the world? A woman.
Who was the cause of a long ten years war,
And laid at last Old-Troy in ashes? Woman.
Destructive, damnable, deceitful woman.

Woman to man first as blessing giv'n,
When innocence and love were in their prime,
Happy a while in Paradise they lay,
But quickly woman long'd to go astray,
Some foolish new adventure needs must prove,
And the first Devil she saw she chang'd her love,
To his temptations lewdly she inclin'd
Her soul, and for an apple damn'd mankind.
Thomas Otway, *The Orphan*, 1680

A man's mind, what there is of it – has always the advantage
of being masculine – as the smallest birch tree is of a higher
kind than the most soaring palm – and even his ignorance is
of a sounder quality.
George Eliot, *Middlemarch*

The more I see of men, the more I admire dogs.
Marie de Rabutin-Chantal, Marquise de Sévigné

You will find that the woman who is really kind to dogs is
always one who has failed to inspire sympathy in men.
Max Beerbohm, *Zuleika Dobson*

. . . So when she's spreading all that
Mess on her face is another good time – do not be shy –
To visit and inspect her. You will find a thousand pots of
    make-up
Colours and grease, that have melted and run
Down into her sweaty cleavage.
Ovid, *Cures for Love*

One of the fathers, if I am rightly informed, has defined a
woman to be an animal that delights in finery. I have . . .

observed, that in all ages they have been more careful than the men to adorn that part of the head which we generally call the outside.

Joseph Addison, in the *Spectator*, 1712

A woman which is fair in show is foul in condition, she is like unto a glow-worm which is bright in the hedge and black in the hand; in the greenest grass lieth hid the greatest serpents; painted pots commonly hold deadly poison; and in the clearest water the ugliest toad: and the fairest woman hath some filthiness in her.

Joseph Swetnam, *Arraignment of Lewd, idle, froward and unconstant women*. This pamphlet led to a play being written about Swetnam in 1619 called *Swetnam the Woman-Hater Arraigned by Women*, in which he gets beaten up by women

English women are elegant until they are ten years old, and perfect on grand occasions.

Nancy Mitford

Take a close-up of a woman past sixty! You might as well use a picture of a relief map of Ireland!

Nancy Astor, when asked for a close-up photograph. Attrib.

My mother used to say it was a great relief to her being an old woman because men left her alone.

Jill Nicholls, in *Spare Rib*

Men are creatures with two legs and eight hands.

Jayne Mansfield

Give a man a free hand and he'll run it all over you.

Mae West

If, sir, I possessed the power of conveying unlimited sexual attraction through the potency of my voice, I would not be reduced to accepting a miserable pittance from the BBC for interviewing a faded female in a damp basement.
Gilbert Harding to Mae West's manager, who suggested he should be more 'sexy' when interviewing her

Let us love dogs; let us love only dogs! Men and cats are unworthy creatures.
Maria Bashkirtseff

There is but one thing in the world worse than a shameless woman, and that's another woman.
Aristophanes, *Thesmophoriazusae*

I used to be Snow White . . . but I drifted.
Mae West

She's the original good time that was had by all.
Bette Davis on the starlet of the time

Mme de Genlis, in order to avoid the scandal of coquetry, always yielded easily.
Talleyrand

Lady Capricorn, he understood, was still keeping open bed.
Aldous Huxley, *Antic Hay*

She's the sort of woman who lives for others – you can always tell the others by their hunted expression.
C. S. Lewis, *The Screwtape Letters*

Madame, you must really be more careful. Suppose it had been someone else who found you like this.
Armand-Emmanuel du Plessis, Duc de Richelieu, when he discovered his wife with her lover

She's like the old line about justice – not only must be done but must be seen to be done.
John Osborne, *Time Present*

You were born with your legs apart. They'll send you to the grave in a Y-shaped coffin.
Joe Orton, *What the Butler Saw*

If the girls at a Yale weekend were laid end to end I wouldn't be a bit surprised.
Dorothy Parker

She is chaste whom nobody has asked.
Ovid, *Amores*, 1.8

A homely face and no figure have aided many women heavenward.
Minna Antrim, *Naked Truth and Veiled Allusions*

Ladies, just a little more virginity, if you don't mind.
Herbert Beerbohm Tree, directing a group of actresses

Age cannot wither her, nor custom stale her infinite virginity.
Daniel Webster, paraphrasing a line from Shakespeare's *Antony and Cleopatra* on hearing of Andrew Jackson's steadfast maintenance that his friend Peggy Eaton did not deserve her scandalous reputation

. . . your virginity, your old virginity, is like one of our French wither'd pears: it looks ill, it eats drily . . .
William Shakespeare, *All's Well That Ends Well*

Sara could commit adultery at one end and weep for her sins at the other, and enjoy both operations at once.
Joyce Cary, *The Horse's Mouth*

Prostitution gives her an opportunity to meet people. It provides fresh air and wholesome exercise, and it keeps her out of trouble.
Joseph Heller, *Catch 22*

You can lead a whore to culture but you can't make her think.
Dorothy Parker, in a speech to the American Horticultural Society

Masculinity and stupidity are often indistinguishable.
H. L. Mencken, *In Defence of Women*, 'The Feminine Mind'

A woman is only a woman,
But a good cigar is a smoke.
Rudyard Kipling; later used by Groucho Marx

Women have many faults, men have only two:
Everything they say, and everything they do.
Anonymous

A woman's place is in the wrong.
James Thurber

Men are nicotine-stained, beer-besmirched, whiskey-greased, red-eyed devils.
Carry Nation

Women are natural bitches.
John Carlisle, MP

The only difference between men is the colour of their neckties.
Helen Broderick in *Top Hat*

Men's men: be they gentle or simple, they're very much of a muchness.
George Eliot, *Daniel Deronda*

I've never found brawn appealing. If I went out with Macho Man I think I'd have a permanent headache. Kind of 'You Tarzan – Mi-graine'.
Overheard on a bus. Quoted in *Picking on Men* by Judy Allen

Whatever women do they must do twice as well as men to be thought half as good. Luckily, this is not difficult.
Charlotte Whitton

The five worst infirmities that afflict the female are indocility, discontent, slander, jealousy, and silliness.
Confucian Marriage Manual

Women want mediocre men, and men are working to be as mediocre as possible.
Margaret Mead

Why are women ... so much more interesting to men than men are to women?
Virginia Woolf, *A Room of One's Own*

Once you know what women are like, men get kind of boring. I'm not trying to put them down, I mean I like some of them sometimes as people, but sexually they're dull.
Rita Mae Brown

The only thing that can make a woman feel lonelier than a vibrator can make her feel is a man.
Isha Elafi

To call man an animal is to flatter him; he's a machine, a walking dildo.
Valerie Solanas, in *S. C. U. M. Manifesto*

The male is a biological accident: the Y (male) chromosome is an incomplete X (female) chromosome, that is, has an incomplete set of genes. In other words, the male is an incomplete female, a walking abortion, aborted at the chromosome stage.
Valerie Solanas, in *S. C. U. M. Manifesto*

Man ... is an afterthought of creation: he is simply a modification of the female.
Deborah Moggach, reviewing *The Redundant Male* by Jeremy Cherfas and John Gribbin, in the *Sunday Times*

A woman without a man is like a fish without a bicycle.
Florynce Kennedy and Gloria Steinem

I will rather trust a Fleming with my butter, Parson Hugh the Welshman with my cheese, an Irishman with my aqua-vitae bottle, or a thief to walk my ambling gelding, than my wife with herself.
William Shakespeare, *The Merry Wives of Windsor*

Bachelors begin at thirty-six. Up till this time they are regarded as single men. Most of them are very tidy, smell of mothballs,

and have an obsessional old maid's fix about one of their ashtrays being moved an inch to the right.
Jilly Cooper, *Men and Super Men*

Because women can do nothing except love, they've given it a ridiculous importance.
W. Somerset Maugham, *The Moon and Sixpence*

By the time you swear you're his,
   Shivering and sighing,
And he vows his passion is
   Infinite, undying –
Lady, make a note of this:
   One of you is lying.
Dorothy Parker, *Enough Rope*, 'Unfortunate Coincidence'

How alike are the groans of love to those of the dying.
Malcolm Lowry, *Under the Volcano*

Girls bored me – they still do. I love Mickey Mouse more than any woman I've ever known.
Walt Disney

Madame: I was told that you took the trouble to come here to see me three times last evening. I was not in. And, fearing lest persistence expose you to humiliation, I am bound by the rules of politeness to warn you that *I shall never be in.*
Gustave Flaubert in a letter to Louise Colet, his former mistress. Colet scribbled on the note '*lâche, couard et canaille*'

O, she is the antidote to desire.
William Congreve, *The Way of the World*

I wonder why men can get serious at all. They have this delicate long thing hanging outside their bodies, which goes up and down by its own will. First of all, having it outside your body is terribly dangerous. If I were a man I would have a fantastic castration complex to the point that I wouldn't be able to do a thing. Second, the inconsistency of it, like carrying a chance time alarm or something. If I were a man I would always be laughing at myself.

Yoko Ono, *On Film No. 4*

To embrace a woman is to embrace a sack of manure.

Odo of Cluny

No longer from head to foot than from hip to hip, she is spherical like a globe; I could find out countries in her.

In what part of her body stands Ireland?

Marry, sir, in her buttocks; I found it out by the bogs.

Where Scotland?

I found it by the barrenness, hard in the palm of the hand.

Where France?

In her forehead, armed and reverted, making war against her heir.

Where England?

I looked for the chalky cliffs, but I could find no whiteness in them. But I guess it stood in her chin, by the salt rheum that ran between France and it.

Where Spain?

Faith, I saw it not; but I felt it hot in her breath.

Where America, the Indies?

O, sir, upon her nose, all o'er embellished with rubies, carbuncles, sapphires, declining their rich aspect to the hot breath of Spain, who sent whole armadas of carracks to be ballast at her nose.

Where stood Belgia, the Netherlands?

O, sir, I did not look so low.

William Shakespeare, *The Comedy of Errors*

... our English gentle-women are now growne so farre past shame, past modesty, grace and nature, as to clip their haire like men with lockes and foretops, and to make this whorish cut the very guise and fashion of the times, to the eternall infamy of their sex, their Nation, and the great scandall of religion.

William Prynne on the seventeenth-century fashion of short hair

Armies of men, herds really, with cameras at the ready, stampeded ... to observe sweet-natured, patient women whose bodies are shaped in a manner that you hardly ever see in the course of normal life. Fat, balding, ugly, drunken, uncouth and deeply unattractive men with flashlights tell these exquisite women what to do and the women do it.

Stephen Pile on topless models promoting motor bikes, in the *Sunday Times*

A woman with a heavily lived-in face poised unceremoniously on top of a torso like a dressmaker's dummy.

Paul Johnson on Lynn Barber, in the *Spectator*

A red-haired, red-faced man of 65 seemingly in transit between Dr Jekyll and Mr Hyde.

Peter McKay on Paul Johnson, in the *Sunday Times*, 7 November 1993

Probably the only place where a man can feel really secure is in a maximum security prison, except for the imminent threat of release.

Germaine Greer, *The Female Eunuch*

The flashers, grabbers, bottom-pinchers, purse-snatchers, kerb-crawlers, verbal abusers, peeping Toms and the ultimate cowards, the ones who roam in packs, have left an indelible impression on women's minds and – more in anger than in fear – women are determined to evade, forestall and undermine these invaders of our freedom.

Valerie Grove, in the *Evening Standard*

The Queen is most anxious to enlist every one who can speak or write to join in checking this mad, wicked folly of 'Woman's Rights', with all its attendant horrors, on which her poor feeble sex is bent, forgetting every sense of womanly feeling and propriety.

Queen Victoria

No *man*, not even a doctor, ever gives any other definition of what a nurse should be than this – 'devoted and obedient'. This definition would do just as well for a porter. It might even do for a horse. It would not do for a policeman.

Florence Nightingale

The legend of the jungle heritage and the evolution of man as a hunting carnivore has taken root in man's mind ... He may even believe that equal pay will do something terrible to his gonads.

Elaine Morgan, *The Descent of Woman*

An open invitation to any feminist, any harridan or any rattle-

headed female with a chip on her bra strap to take action against her employers.
Tony Marlow, MP, on equal-pay law

A gentleman is a patient wolf.
Henrietta Tiarks

Certain women should be struck regularly, like gongs.
Noël Coward, *Private Lives*

Homosexuality is a sickness, just as are baby-rape or wanting to become the head of General Motors.
Eldridge Cleaver, black Muslim, *Soul on Ice*, 'Notes on a Native Son'

He is the summit of sex, the pinnacle of masculine, feminine and neuter. Everything that he, she and it can ever want.

I spoke to sad but kindly men on this newspaper who have met every celebrity coming from America for the past thirty years. They say that this deadly, winking, sniggering, snuggling, chromium-plated, scent-impregnated, luminous, quivering, giggling, fruit-flavoured, mincing, ice-covered, heap of mother love has had the biggest reception and impact on London since Charlie Chaplin arrived at the same station, Waterloo, on September 12th 1921.

This appalling man, and I use the word appalling in no other than its true sense of terrifying, has hit this country in a way that is as violent as Churchill receiving the cheers on VE Day.

He reeks of emetic language that can only make grown men long for a quiet corner, an aspidistra, a handkerchief and the old heave-ho. Without doubt he is the biggest sentimental vomit of all time. Slobbering over his Mother, winking at his brother, and counting the cash at every second, this superb piece of calculating candyfloss has an answer for every situation.

'Cassandra' on Liberace, in the *Daily Mirror*. This piece was the subject of a famous libel case won by the entertainer

I became one of the stately homos of England.

Quentin Crisp, *The Naked Civil Servant*

A bull who would copulate only with other bulls would be sent to the knackers.

Piers Paul Read, in *The Times*, 1994

This sort of thing may be tolerated by the French, but we are British – thank God.

Viscount Montgomery of Alamein on the proposed relaxation of laws against homosexuality in 1965

If Michelangelo had been a heterosexual, the Sistine Chapel would have been painted basic white and with a roller.

Rita Mae Brown on Michelangelo

We know of course that women are habitually constipated, but to represent them in fiction as being altogether devoid of a back passage seems to me really an excess of chivalry.

W. Somerset Maugham, *Cakes and Ale*

When his cock wouldn't stand up he blew his head off. He sold himself a line of bullshit, and bought it.

Germaine Greer on Ernest Hemingway

The trouble with Ian is that he gets off with women because he can't get on with them.

Rosamond Lehmann on Ian Fleming

They are comforted by our means; they are nourished by the meats we dress; their bodies freed from diseases by our cleanliness, which otherwise would surfeit unreasonably through their own noisomeness. Without our care they lie in their beds as dogs in litter and go like lousy mackerel swimming in the heat of summer.

Jane Anger, *Her Protection for Women*, 1589

Except in streetcars one should never be unnecessarily rude to a lady.

O. Henry, *Strictly Business*, 'The Gold That Glittered'

The fastest way to a man's heart is through his chest.

Roseanne Barr

Gout is very much in my line, gentlemen are not.

Dr Elizabeth Garrett Anderson, letter to a man hoping to be treated for gout

Female violence has increased by 192% in ten years. Other women, of course, have joined the League Against Cruel Sports or become lesbians and gone to Greenham Common. This is the sort of thing you must expect when you stop treating them as sex objects.

Auberon Waugh, in *Private Eye*, 1983

It makes me feel masculine to tell you that I do not answer questions like this without being paid for answering them.

Lillian Hellman, when asked by *Harper's Magazine* when she felt most masculine

Many a man has been a wonder to the world, whose wife and

valet have seen nothing in him that was even remarkable. Few men have been admired by their servants.
Michel de Montaigne, *Essais*, III

No man is a hero to his valet.
Anne-Marie Bigot de Cornuel

But that is not because the hero is no hero, but because the valet is a valet.
Friedrich Nietzsche

A fly, Sir, may sting a stately horse and make him wince; but one is but an insect, and the other is still a horse.
Samuel Johnson

Brigands demand your money or your life; women require both.
Samuel Butler. Attrib.

A woman will always sacrifice herself if you give her the opportunity. It is her favourite form of self-indulgence.
W. Somerset Maugham, *The Circle*

Well, what all-American hero wouldn't send his wife in for surgery rather than himself?
Dr Bernard Levatin, urologist, when asked by a news reporter why female sterilization was more common when vasectomies were cheaper, faster, possibly safer, and just as effective

Damn the North! and damn the South! and damn Wellington! the question is, how am I going to get rid of this damned Princess of Wales.
Prince of Wales, later George IV, on a political marriage for him despite his private marriage to Mrs Fitzherbert

A sort of friendship recognized by the police.
Robert Louis Stevenson on matrimony

Nothing is to me more distasteful than that entire complacency and satisfaction which beam in the countenances of a new-married couple.
Charles Lamb, *Essays of Elia*, 'A Bachelor's Complaint of Married People'

'We stay together, but we distrust one another.'
'Ah, yes ... but isn't that a definition of marriage?'
Malcolm Bradbury, *The History Man*

It was very good of God to let Carlyle and Mrs Carlyle marry one another and so make only two people miserable instead of four.
Samuel Butler on the Carlyles

Marriage is like a cage: one sees the birds outside desperate to get in, and those inside equally desperate to get out.
Michel de Montaigne, *Essais*, III

There are two tragedies in life. One is to lose your heart's desire. The other is to gain it.
George Bernard Shaw

Courtship to marriage, as a very witty prologue to a very dull Play.
William Congreve, *The Old Bachelor*

A man in love is incomplete until he has married. Then he's finished.
Zsa Zsa Gabor

The most happy marriage I can picture or imagine to myself
would be the union of a deaf man and a blind woman.
Samuel Taylor Coleridge

All tragedies are finish'd by a death,
All comedies are ended by a marriage.
Lord Byron, *Don Juan*, III

A woman's silly, never staid,
By many longings stirred and swayed.
If husband can't her needs supply,
Adultery's the way she'll try . . .

Her lustful loins are never stilled:
By just one man she's unfulfilled.
She'll spread her legs to all the men
But, ever hungry, won't say 'When'.

Thus married women love to stray
And wish their husbands' lives away.
Since none a woman's lust can sate
I don't commend the marriage state.

De Coniuge non Ducenda, anonymous poem on marriage, *c.*1225–50. One of
the most popular anti-matrimonial satires of the later Middle Ages. Survives
in over fifty manuscripts.

As I roll back from you,
from your flabby breasts and breath,
a faint froth is our only link.

How many beaches are you?
Must I comb them all?

I'm not a wave to roll again forever,
and unlike the sea,
I don't come
every fifteen seconds.
Jim Lindsey, 'Blank Verse for a Fat Demanding Wife'

The majority of husbands remind me of an orang-utan trying
to play the violin.
Honoré de Balzac

Mrs Hall of Sherbourne was brought to bed yesterday of a
dead child, some weeks before she expected, owing to a fright.
I suppose she happened to look unawares at her husband.
Jane Austen, letter

You will be amused with John Murray's marriage ... Ten days
finished the matter; indeed she has no time to lose, since she
is 39. I never saw two longer fatter lovers, for she is as big as
Murray. They looked enormous as they were making love in
the plantations ... Seriously speaking it is a very good marriage, and acting under the direction of medical men, with
perseverance and the use of stimulating diet, there may be an
heir to the house of Henderland.
Sydney Smith on a forthcoming marriage

Going to marry her! Going to marry her! Impossible! You
mean, a part of her; he could not marry her all himself. It
would be a case, not of bigamy, but of trigamy; the neighbourhood or the magistrates should interfere. There is enough
of her to furnish wives for a whole parish. One man marry
her! – it is monstrous. You might people a colony with her;
or give an assembly with her; or perhaps take your morning

walks around her, always providing there were frequent resting places, and you are in rude health. I once was rash enough to try walking round her before breakfast, but only got half-way and gave it up exhausted. Or you might read the Riot Act and disperse her; in short, you might do anything with her but marry her.
Sydney Smith on hearing that a young man planned to marry a fat widow

A man . . . is *so* in the way in the house.
Elizabeth Gaskell, *Cranford*

The cloy of all pleasure, the luggage of life,
Is the best that can be said for a very good wife.
John Wilmot, Earl of Rochester

To lose a lover or even a husband or two during the course of one's life can be vexing. But to lose one's teeth is a catastrophe.
Hugh Wheeler

Here lies my wife; here let her lie!
Now she's at rest, and so am I.
John Dryden, 'Epitaph Intended for Dryden's Wife'

Bigamy is having one husband too many. Monogamy is the same.
Anonymous, quoted in Erica Jong, *Fear of Flying*

With all my heart. Whose wife shall it be?
John Horne Tooke, replying to the suggestion that he take a wife

I give to Elizabeth Parker the sum of £50, whom, through my foolish fondness, I made my wife; and who in return has

not spared, most unjustly, to accuse me of every crime regarding human nature, save highway-robbery.
Charles Parker, excerpt from will, 1785

I do give and bequeath to Mary Davis the sum of five shillings, which is sufficient to enable her to get drunk for the last time at my expense.
David Davis, excerpt from will, 1788

There are few who would not rather be taken in adultery than in provincialism.
Aldous Huxley, *Antic Hay*

It should be a very happy marriage – they are both so much in love with *him*.
Irene Thomas

You have sent me a Flanders mare.
Henry VIII when he saw Anne of Cleves, his fourth wife, for the first time.
Quoted by Tobias Smollett

I like him and his wife. He is so ladylike, and she is such a perfect gentleman.
Sydney Smith

All my wife has ever taken from the Mediterranean – from that whole vast intuitive culture – are four bottles of Chianti to make into lamps, and two china condiment donkeys labelled Sally and Peppy.
Peter Shaffer

I've been married six months. She looks like a million dollars,

but she only knows a hundred and twenty words and she's only got two ideas in her head. The other one's hats.
Eric Linklater, *Juan in America*

She is an excellent creature, but never can remember which came first, the Greeks or the Romans.
Benjamin Disraeli on his wife. Attrib.

. . . fools are as like husbands as pilchards are to herrings; the husband's the bigger.
William Shakespeare, *Twelfth Night*

Twenty years of romance makes a woman look like a ruin; but twenty years of marriage makes her something like a public building.
Oscar Wilde

I married beneath me – all women do.
Nancy Astor

There are only about 20 murders a year in London and not all are serious – some are just husbands killing their wives.
Commander G. H. Hatherill of Scotland Yard, 1954

Divorce! Never. But murder often!
Dame Sybil Thorndike, asked whether she had ever considered divorce during her marriage to Lewis Casson

They fuck you up, your mum and dad.
    They may not mean to, but they do.
They fill you with the faults they had
    And add some extra, just for you.
Philip Larkin, 'This Be The Verse'

Do not leave your mother alone with your dog. The unruliness of mothers is great.

Dabi' Ibn al-Harith al-Burjumi on some people to whom he had refused to return a borrowed dog. For this piece of *hija*, or Arabic invective poetry, he was imprisoned

Who has not watched a mother stroke her child's cheek or kiss her child *in a certain way* and felt a nervous shudder at the possessive outrage done to a free solitary human soul?

John Cowper Powys, *The Meaning of Culture*

His mother should have thrown him away and kept the stork.

Mae West

Men are generally more careful of the breed of their horses and dogs than of their children.

William Penn

It is no use telling me that there are bad aunts and good aunts. At the core they are all alike. Sooner or later, out pops the cloven hoof.

P. G. Wodehouse, *The Code of the Woosters*

I am, sir, for the last time in my life, Your Humble Servant Horace Walpole.

Horace Walpole, ending a letter to an uncle with whom he had recently quarrelled

From the earliest times the old have rubbed it into the young that they are wiser than they, and before the young had discovered what nonsense this was they were old too, and it profited them to carry on the imposture.

W. Somerset Maugham, *Cakes and Ale*

I have lived some thirty years on this planet, and I have yet to hear the first syllable of valuable or even earnest advice from my seniors.
Henry David Thoreau

At sixteen I was stupid, confused, insecure and indecisive. At twenty-five I was wise, self-confident, prepossessing and assertive. At forty-five I am stupid, confused, insecure and indecisive. Who would have supposed that maturity is only a short break in adolescence?
Jules Feiffer

Whenever a man's friends begin to compliment him about looking young, he may be sure that they think he is growing old.
Washington Irving, *Bracebridge Hall*, 'Bachelors'

The three ages of man: youth, middle age, and 'You're looking well, Enoch!'
Enoch Powell, on being told he looked well

The young always have the same problem – how to rebel and conform at the same time. They have now solved this by defying their parents and copying one another.
Quentin Crisp, *The Naked Civil Servant*

Look, the intellects of our lazy youth are asleep, nor do they wake up for the exercise of a single respectable occupation; slumber and languor and, what is more disgusting than slumber and languor, the pursuit of wicked things has invaded their spirit: the obscene pursuit of singing and dancing keeps them effeminate, and curling the hair and shrilling the voice into womanish cajoleries, competing with women in the softness of the body and cultivating themselves with the foulest elegances, that is the pattern of our young men. Who of your agemates is what I might call intellectual enough, diligent enough, rather, who is enough of a man? Softened up and emasculate as they were born they remain all their lives, laying siege to other people's chastity, careless of their own.

Seneca, first century BC, *Controversiae*, I, Introduction, on the youth of his day. Tr. Amy Richlin

'Old Cary Grant fine. How you?

Cary Grant, replying to a telegram to his agent which asked: 'How old Cary Grant?'

I am just turning forty and taking my time about it.

Harold Lloyd at seventy-seven, when asked his age, in *The Times*

Do you think my mind is maturing late,
Or simply rotted early?

Ogden Nash

The misery of a child is interesting to a Mother, the misery of a young man is interesting to a young woman, the misery of an old man is interesting to no one.

Victor Hugo, *Les Misérables*, 'Saint Denis'

Poor old Daddy — just one of those sturdy old plants left over from the Edwardian Wilderness, that can't understand why the sun isn't shining any more.

John Osborne, *Look Back in Anger*

There are one hundred and ninety-three living species of monkeys and apes. One hundred and ninety-two of them are

covered with hair. The exception is a naked ape self-named
Homo sapiens.
Desmond Morris, *The Naked Ape*

Drinking when we are not thirsty and making love all year
round, madam; that is all there is to distinguish us from other
animals.
Pierre-Augustin Caron de Beaumarchais, *Le Mariage de Figaro*

The human race, to which so many of my readers belong.
G. K. Chesterton

Society is now one polish'd horde,
Form'd of two mighty tribes, the *Bores* and *Bored.*
Lord Byron, *Don Juan,* XIII

Style, like sheer silk, too often hides eczema.
Albert Camus, *The Fall*

Man, as he is, is not a genuine article. He is an imitation of
something, and a very bad imitation.
P. D. Ouspensky

No one ever lacks a good reason for suicide.
Cesare Pavese, who committed suicide in 1950

No arts; no letters; no society; and which is worst of all,
continual fear and danger of violent death; and the life of
man, solitary, poor, nasty, brutish, and short.
Thomas Hobbes, *Leviathan*

Have I not reason to hate and to despise myself? Indeed I do;

and chiefly for not having hated and despised the world enough.
William Hazlitt, 'On the Pleasure of Hating'

The belief in the supernatural source of evil is not necessary; men alone are quite capable of every wickedness.
Joseph Conrad, *Under Western Eyes*

Man is the only animal that blushes. Or needs to.
Mark Twain

Man is the only animal that can remain on friendly terms with the victims he intends to eat until he eats them.
Samuel Butler

I wish I loved the Human Race;
I wish I loved its silly face;
I wish I liked the way it walks;
I wish I liked the way it talks;
And when I'm introduced to one
I wish I thought *What Jolly Fun!*
Sir Walter Alexander Raleigh, *Laughter from a Cloud*, 'Wishes of an Elderly Man'

The world itself is but a large prison, out of which some are daily led to execution.
Sir Walter Ralegh, after his trial for treason. Attrib.

I am told I am a true cosmopolitan. I am unhappy everywhere.
Stephen Vizinczey, in the *Guardian*

Man is a noble animal, splendid in ashes, and pompous in the grave.
Sir Thomas Browne

One has often wondered whether upon the whole earth there is anything so unintelligent, so unapt to perceive how the world is really going, as an ordinary young Englishman of our upper classes.
Matthew Arnold, *Culture and Anarchy*

The king blew his nose twice, and wiped the royal perspiration repeatedly from a face which is probably the largest uncivilized spot in England.
Oliver Wendell Holmes on William IV

Good-morning, gentlemen both.
Elizabeth I, addressing a group of eighteen tailors

To promote a Woman to beare rule, superioritie, dominion, or empire above any Realme, nation, or Citie, is repugnant to Nature; contumelie to God, a thing most contrarious to his reveled will and approved ordinance; and finallie, it is the subversion of good Order, of all equitie and justice ... For who can denie but it is repugneth to nature, that the blind shall be appointed to leade and conduct such as do see? That the weake, the sicke, and impotent persons shall norishe and kepe the hole and the strong? And finallie, that the foolishe, madde, and phrenetike shall governe the discrete, and give counsel to such as be of sober mind? Of such be all women, compared unto man in bearing of authoritie. For their sight in civile regiment is but blindnes; their strength, weaknes; their counsel, foolishnes; and judgment, phrensie, if it be rightlie considered ...
John Knox, *First Blast of the Trumpet against the Monstrous Regiment of Women*. Knox attacks various women rulers hostile to the Reformation: Catherine de' Medici, Mary of Guise, and above all Mary Tudor. But by generalizing

about all women, it offended Elizabeth I, a potentially powerful pro-Reformation figure, when she ascended to the throne. Knox tried to apologize in a letter to Sir William Cecil ('I had no suspicion of the book, and for a whole year was ignorant of its publication'), but Elizabeth remained unappeased.

The most notorious whore in all the world.
Peter Wentworth on Mary, Queen of Scots

Anne ... when in good humour, was meekly stupid, and when in bad humour, was sulkily stupid.
Thomas Babington Macaulay on Queen Anne

The wisest fool in Christendom.
Henri IV, first Bourbon King of France, on James I of England. Attrib.

An old, mad, blind, despised, and dying king –
Princes, the dregs of their dull race, who flow
Through public scorn – mud from a muddy spring;
Rulers who neither see, nor feel, nor know,
But leechlike to their fainting country cling,
Till they drop, blind in blood, without a blow ...
Percy Bysshe Shelley on George III, his family and Government, 'England in 1819'. Shelley wrote the piece after troops attacked a crowd of unarmed protesters, killing several, who were demonstrating in Manchester in favour of parliamentary reform

The Radical MP John Wilkes at a formal dinner in the presence of the Prince of Wales proposed a toast to the King's health, a thing which no one had ever known him do before. The Prince asked Wilkes how long he had shown such concern for his father's well-being. Wilkes replied: 'Since I had the pleasure of your Royal Highness's acquaintance.'
John Wilkes on the Prince of Wales, later George IV

Who's your fat friend?
George 'Beau' Brummell to Beau Nash, who had introduced the Prince Regent

Nowadays, a parlour maid as ignorant as Queen Victoria was when she came to the throne, would be classed as mentally defective.
George Bernard Shaw on Queen Victoria

Sir,
I am loth to interrupt the rapture of mourning in which the nation is now enjoying its favourite festival – a funeral. But in a country like ours the total suspension of common sense and sincere human feeling for a whole fortnight is an impossibility.
A letter from George Bernard Shaw to the *Morning Leader* after the death of Queen Victoria. The editor declined to publish the letter

Very sorry can't come. Lie follows by post.
Telegram from Charles Beresford to the Prince of Wales, later Edward VIII, following a dinner invitation at short notice

I don't mind your being killed, but I object to your being taken prisoner.
Lord Kitchener to the Prince of Wales, when he asked to go to the Western Front in the First World War

No thank you; I only smoke on special occasions.
Anonymous commoner, confused and overawed, on being asked by George VI at a banquet whether he cared for a cigar

He will go from resort to resort getting more tanned and more tired.
Westbrook Pegler on the abdication of Edward VIII, quoted by Alistair Cooke, *Six Men*

God grant him peace and happiness but never understanding of what he has lost.
Stanley Baldwin on the abdication of Edward VIII

The Billy Carter of the British monarchy.
Robert Lacey on Princess Margaret

[A] wife capable of behaving in this way: tantrums and suicide charades – anyone trying to do it with paracetamol isn't trying – is a witless little girl unfit for marriage to anyone. And the wife capable of exploiting her position to get revenge through mass publicity is a destructive little chancer emotionally located in the foothills of adolescence. The footling story of Diana Spencer makes a bitter republican point, the liability of fairy tales to have been written by the Brothers Grimm! . . .

Charles has claims to be a victim of the Asiatic fixing of his family. No wife brought from Karachi to Southall by imperious parents-in-law could better represent an arranged marriage than the English rose heavily urged for the Crown Prince. She was English (after much public scorn of the former Teutonic norm), a virgin and thus free from all tattle, and she looked good. The facts: that she is a virtuoso of on-camera tears, that her delight in life is the nightclub and that she seems to have no mind at all, were disregarded. An intelligent man has been fettered in 'a suitable marriage' to a frothball and has sought to live his life apart from her. What sharper intimation of the shabbiness of monarchy could there be?

There are many reasons for dispensing with monarchy, but

two will suffice. The job could be done better; and monarchy, just by existing, induces pathetic impulses in other people. There has to be something wrong with an institution which assembles, in various degrees of competitive abjectness, Lord St John of Fawsley, in whom I have real difficulty believing, Sir Alastair Burnet and Lord Rees-Mogg.

These Firbankian grotesques, prime fruit of the tree of deference, can be relied upon to squelch noisily under royal foot. Happy calling someone twenty years younger 'Sir' or 'Maa-am', they proclaim a social pyramid in which their own status is secured by guileful proximity to the apex. They fawn and teach us to fawn. Unlike the late Richard Dimbleby, grand under-butler to the nation, they do not tell us that the Queen looks radiant, but they are lit by all the royal reflection into which they can creep.

Such courtiers only echo the sick adoration of part of the nation. Royalty has done a roaring trade since the war in glossy iconic tosh, books about royal lives, houses, tours, weddings, ancestry and interior décors, books, God help us, about royal dogs. The appetite of silly people for living vicarious, reverential lives through this assembly of low-octane duds in jodhpurs is tragic.

Edward Pearce, *Guardian*, 'The Aspirin of the People'

Prince Charles is an insensitive, hypocritical oaf and Princess Diana is a selfish, empty-headed bimbo. They should never have got married in the first place. I blame the parents.

Richard Littlejohn, in the *Sun*

Michael Shea, the Queen's former press secretary, claims he hasn't read the *Sun* since he left Buck House in 1987 . . . that hasn't prevented him passing damning judgement on the 'gutter press'.

From his new, exalted position £120,000 up Lord Hanson's backside, Shea pours bile and contempt on the tabloids, the people who work for them and the people who read them . . .

We stand accused of lack of deference, prurience and down-right spiteful invention . . .

Lack of deference? Rather that than a forelock-tugging flunkey.

Prurience? No more so than readers of the *Observer* who queued round the block for a full-frontal gander at Madonna's naughty bits.

Spiteful invention? No one is trying to pretend that the papers don't get it wrong from time to time . . . Reporters would get things wrong less often if people like Shea told the truth.

'The intention was always to be helpful and forthcoming to all concerned,' Shea writes in *The Times* . . .

Shea was a master of evasion, more slippery than a Jacuzzi full of KY Jelly. You might say he was the first Sensitol-lubricated PR man – particularly appropriate when you consider where he has spent most of his life.

Royal reporters say meeting Shea was like shaking hands with a bar of wet soap. Except you come away feeling clean when you shake hands with a bar of wet soap.

Perhaps if Shea had been more open and honest – if he had given Her Majesty better advice – matters would not have come to quite the unpleasant head they have recently.

I bear no personal animosity towards the Royals and I suspect few other people do.

It is the Sir Alan Fitztightlys of this world, the bowing and scraping courtiers like Shea, who consider themselves above the common herd by virtue of their employer, that I can't abide...

Richard Littlejohn on Michael Shea, the Queen's former press secretary, in the *Sun*

I'm prepared to take advice on leisure from Prince Philip. He's a world expert on leisure. He's been practising for most of his adult life.

Neil Kinnock on Prince Philip, in the *Western Mail*

She is a lady short on looks, absolutely deprived of any dress sense, has a figure like a Jurassic monster, [seems] very greedy when it comes to loot, no tact and wants to upstage everyone else.

Sir Nicholas Fairbairn on Sarah, the Duchess of York, in the *Independent*

Why don't you naff off!

Princess Anne to reporters, in the *Daily Mirror*

Actually I vote Labour, but my butler's a Tory.

Earl Mountbatten to a canvasser during the 1945 election

The difference between us is that my family begins with me, whereas yours ends with you.

Iphicrates, Athenian general and the son of a cobbler, replying to a descendant of the Athenian hero Harmodius who had mocked his lowly origins

Of course they have, or I wouldn't be talking to you.

Barbara Cartland, when asked by BBC reporter Sandra Harris in a radio interview whether she thought English class barriers had broken down

Aristocrats spend their childhood being beaten by fierce

nannies and their later years murdering wildlife, so it's hardly
surprising their sex lives are a bit cock-eyed.
Jilly Cooper, *Men and Super Men*

An aristocracy in a republic is like a chicken whose head has
been cut off: it may run about in a lively way, but in fact it is
dead.
Nancy Mitford, *Noblesse Oblige*

Sacred to the memory of
Captain Anthony Wedgwood
Accidentally shot by his gamekeeper
Whilst out shooting
'Well done thou good and faithful servant'
Epitaph

How beastly the bourgeois is
especially the male of the species – . . .

Nicely groomed, like a mushroom
standing there so sleek and erect and eyeable –
and like a fungus, living on the remains of bygone life
sucking his life out of the dead leaves of greater life than his
    own.

And even so, he's stale, he's been there too long.
Touch him, and you'll find he's all gone inside
just like an old mushroom, all wormy inside, and hollow
under a smooth skin and an upright appearance.

Full of seething, wormy, hollow feelings
rather nasty –
How beastly the bourgeois is!

Standing in their thousands, these appearances, in damp
   England
what a pity they can't all be kicked over
like sickening toadstools, and left to melt back, swiftly
into the soil of England.

D. H. Lawrence, *Pansies*, 'How beastly the bourgeois is'

But that vast portion, lastly, of the working-class which, raw
and half-developed, has long lain half-hidden amidst its
poverty and squalor, and is now issuing from its hiding place
to assert an Englishman's heaven-born privilege of doing as
he likes, and is beginning to perplex us by marching where it
likes, meeting where it likes, bawling what it likes, breaking
what it likes – to this vast residuum we may with great
propriety give the name of Populace.

Matthew Arnold, *Culture and Anarchy*

Walk through her cities, walk with a pal
Through the streets between the power-house and green canal
And see what they're at – our proletariat.
O my, what peeps
At disheartened sweeps –
Fitters and moulders,
Wielders and welders,
Dyers and bakers
And boiler-tube makers,
Poufs and ponces,
All of them dunces.
Those over thirty,
Ugly and dirty,
What are they doing

Except just stewing?
Content for the year
With foods out of tins and very small beer –
Flaking the rust off obsolete plant
Slacking at the corners thinking 'I can't.'
Sloping up the hill, for they've nowhere else to go –
To the park and the platforms where the windbags blow
Spying on athletes playing on a green,
Spying on kisses shown on a screen,
Their minds as pathic as a boxer's face,
A shamed, uninteresting, and hopeless race.

W. H. Auden on the English classes, 'Birthday Ode'

Poverty is an anomaly to rich people. It is very difficult to make out why people who want dinner do not ring the bell.

Walter Bagehot

Let them eat cake.

Marie-Antoinette repeating an old saying, when told that the people had no bread to eat

MY LORD, – Now I am recovering from an illness of several months' duration, aggravated no little by your lordship's rude reception of me at the Cascine, in presence of my family and innumerable Florentines. I must remind you in the gentlest terms of the occurrence.

We are both of us old men, my lord, and are verging on decrepitude and imbecility. Else my note might be more energetic. I am not unobservant of distinctions. You, by the favour of a minister, are Marquis of Normanby, I by the grace of God am

WALTER SAVAGE LANDOR

W. S. Landor, letter to Lord Normanby, who had cut him

Someone has said that the King may make a nobleman, but he cannot make a gentleman.

Edmund Burke

I like the Garter; there is no damned merit in it.

Lord Melbourne

Lady Jane Seymour, the granddaughter of Richard Brinsley Sheridan, had been chosen 'Queen of Beauty' sometime earlier at a pseudo-medieval tournament led by Louis Napoleon. The following is an exchange of correspondence between her and Lady Shuckburgh.

Lady Seymour presents her compliments to Lady Shuckburgh, and would be obliged to her for the character of Mary Stedman, who states that she lived twelve months, and still is, in Lady Shuckburgh's establishment. Can Mary Stedman cook plain dishes well? make bread? and is she honest, good-tempered, sober, willing, and cleanly? Lady Seymour would also like to know the reason why she leaves Lady Shuckburgh's service? Direct, under cover to Lord Seymour, Maiden Bradley.

Lady Shuckburgh presents her compliments to Lady Seymour. Her ladyship's note, dated October 28, only reached her yesterday, November 3. Lady Shuckburgh was unacquainted with the name of the kitchen-maid until mentioned by Lady Seymour, as it is her custom neither to apply for or give characters to any of the under servants, this being always done by the housekeeper, Mrs Couch – and this was well known to the young woman; therefore Lady Shuckburgh is surprised at her referring any lady to her for a character. Lady Shuckburgh having a professed cook, as well as a housekeeper, in her establishment, it is not very likely that she herself should know anything of the abilities or merits of the under servants; therefore she is unable to answer Lady Seymour's note. Lady Shuckburgh cannot imagine Mary Stedman to be capable of cooking for any except the servants'-hall table.

Lady Seymour presents her compliments to Lady Shuckburgh, and begs she will order her housekeeper, Mrs Pouch, to send the girl's character without delay; otherwise another young woman will be sought for elsewhere, as Lady Seymour's children cannot remain without their dinners because Lady Shuckburgh, keeping a 'professed cook and a housekeeper', thinks a knowledge of the details of her establishment beneath her notice. Lady Seymour understands from Stedman that, in addition to her other talents, she was actually capable of dressing food fit for the little Shuckburghs to partake of when hungry.

(Attached to this was a cartoon of the three Shuckburgh children, with large heads and cauliflower wigs, slavering over a chop prepared by a grinning Mary Stedman, while their mother hovered in dismay)

MADAM,

Lady Shuckburgh has directed me to acquaint you that she declines answering your note, the vulgarity of which is beneath contempt; and although it may be the characteristic of the Sheridans to be vulgar, coarse, and witty, it is not that of a 'lady', unless she happens to have been born in a garret and bred in a kitchen. Mary Stedman informs me that your ladyship does not keep either a cook or a housekeeper, and that you only require a girl who can cook a mutton chop. If so, I apprehend that Mary Stedman, or any other scullion, will be found equal to cook for or manage the establishment of the Queen of Beauty. I am, your ladyship, &c.,

    ELIZABETH COUCH (not Pouch).

I've been offered titles, but I think they get one into disreputable company.
George Bernard Shaw

Not really. Experience has taught us that those who matter don't mind and those who mind don't matter.
Ambassador to a dinner guest who had forced her fellow guests to swap seats after discovering precedence ought to accord her a place closer to the Ambassador. She had said to him: 'I expect you find these questions of precedence very troublesome, Your Excellency.'

We invite people like that to tea, but we don't marry them.
Lady Chetwode on her future son-in-law, John Betjeman

What you need is a couple of aspirates.
F. E. Smith to Jimmy Thomas, who never pronounced his h's, after he complained of an 'eadache

No writer before the middle of the 19th century wrote about the working classes other than as grotesque or as pastoral decoration. Then when they were given the vote certain writers started to suck up to them.
Evelyn Waugh

I never knew the working classes had such white skins.
Lord Curzon, seeing some troops bathing during the First World War

We are all beautiful (except white
people, they are full of and made of
shit) . . .
Imamu Amiri Baraka, *Black Magic*, 'A school of prayer'

One of the things that makes a Negro unpleasant to white
folks is the fact that he suffers from their injustice. He is thus
a standing rebuke to them.
H. L. Mencken

[A person is] a male person, including an Indian and excluding
a person of Mongolian or Chinese race.
Canada Franchise Act 1885

Porkie.
Jamaican term of abuse for white people

What negroes want is tight pussy, loose shoes and a warm
place to shit.
Earl Butz, American Secretary of State for Agriculture in the Nixon administration

When the white man is about to leave a garden for good, he
wrecks it.
Yoruba proverb

Making love to a white man is like making love to a skinned
animal.
Anonymous Nigerian woman

The white man knows how to make everything, but he does not know how to distribute it.
Sitting Bull

The natural religion of the Creeks, Cherokees, Chickasaws and all other Indians, is to torture all their prisoners from morning to night, til at length they roast them to death . . .

Yea, it is a common thing among them for the son, if he thinks his father lives too long, to knock out his brains.
John Wesley, *Works*, v

The white race is the cancer of all human history. It is the white race and it alone, its ideologies and inventions, which eradicate autonomous civilizations wherever it spreads.
Susan Sontag, *Partisan Review*

White people say to me 'Isn't there *anything* good about us?' and I reply 'Yes. You sure can ski. You're beautiful skiers.'
Paul Mooney

The Sioux Indians are a set of miserable, dirty, lousy, blanketed, seething, lying, sneaking, murdering, graceless, faceless, dog-eating SKUNKS as the Lord ever permitted to infect the earth, and whose immediate and final extermination all MEN, excepting Indian agents and traders, should pray for.
Topeka Weekly Daily, 1869

I'm a coloured, one-eyed Jew.
Sammy Davis, Jr., when asked what his handicap was during a game of golf

There is only one race greater than the Jews – and that is the Derby.
Victor Sassoon

All those who are not racially pure are mere chaff.
Adolf Hitler, *Mein Kampf*

The gentleman will please remember that when his half-civilized ancestors were hunting the wild boar in Silesia, mine were princes of the earth.
Judah Benjamin, in reply to an anti-Semitic remark by a senator of German origin. Attrib.

He says that I am anti-Semitic – but the reason I don't like him is not because he is Jewish but because I think that he is a nasty little worm.
Alan Clark, the *Guardian* ©

It is extremely difficult for a Jew to be converted, for how can he bring himself to believe in the divinity of – another Jew?
Heinrich Heine

If a Jew can have the rope free of charge he will let himself be hanged.
Russian insult

If the Jew is of gold, his testicles are of copper.
Moorish insult

Lord, I ascribe it to Thy grace,
And not to chance, as others do,
That I was born of Christian race,
And not a Heathen, or a Jew.
English hymn by Isaac Watts, from his *Divine Songs for Children*

. . . a tendency – from which I suffer myself – to presume that

anyone of any eminence at all is Jewish, unless he or she can show definitive proof to the contrary.
Chaim Bermant

No, not really. Except this: We think they're stupid.
Dominic Lawson, when asked at a *Spectator* lunch whether Jews held any prejudice against Gentiles, comparable to anti-Semitism

Few people can be happy unless they hate some other person, nation or creed.
Bertrand Russell

The great nations have always acted like gangsters, and the small nations like prostitutes.
Stanley Kubrick, in the *Guardian*

In Western Europe there are now only small countries – those that know it and those that don't know it yet.
Théo Lefèvre, Belgian Prime Minister

This going into Europe will not turn out to be the thrilling mutual exchange supposed. It is more like nine middle-aged couples with failing marriages meeting in a darkened bedroom in a Brussels hotel for a Group Grope.
E. P. Thompson on the EEC, in the *Sunday Times*, 1975

A small acquaintance with history shows that all Governments are selfish and the French Governments more selfish than most.
Lord Eccles

I do not dislike the French from the vulgar antipathy between

neighbouring nations, but for their insolent and unfounded airs of superiority.
Horace Walpole

In all the four corners of the earth one of these three names is given to him who steals from his neighbour: brigand, robber or Englishman.
Les Triades de l'Anglais

France was a long despotism tempered by epigrams.
Thomas Carlyle, *History of the French Revolution*

Poltroons, cowards, skulkers and dastards.
Eustache Deschamps on the English

France is a dog-hole.
William Shakespeare, *All's Well That Ends Well*

England is a nation of shopkeepers.
Napoleon Bonaparte

The ignorance of French society gives one a rough sense of the infinite.
Joseph E. Renan

They are short, blue-vested people who carry their own onions when cycling abroad, and have a yard which is 3·37 inches longer than other people's.
Alan Coren on the French

France is a country where the money falls apart in your hands and you can't tear the toilet paper.
Billy Wilder

I found there a country with thirty-two religions and only one sauce.

Talleyrand on America

Nobody can simply bring together a country that has 365 kinds of cheese.

Charles de Gaulle on France

It was wonderful to find America, but it would have been more wonderful to miss it.

Mark Twain

Paul Bourget, French novelist: 'Life can never be entirely dull to an American. When he has nothing else to do he can always spend a few years trying to discover who his grandfather was.'

   Mark Twain: 'Right, your Excellency. But I reckon a Frenchman's got a little standby for a dull time too; he can turn in and see if he can find out who his father was.'

Mark Twain

I heard an Englishman, who had been long resident in America, declare that in following, in meeting, or in over-taking, in the street, on the road, or in the field, at the theatre, the coffee-house, or at home, he had never overheard Americans conversing without the word DOLLAR being pronounced between them. Such unity of purpose . . . can . . . be found nowhere else, except . . . in an ant's nest.

Frances Trollope, *A Commentary on Travels on a Mississippi Steamer*

America is the only nation in history which miraculously has gone from barbarism to degeneration without the usual interval of civilization.

Georges Clemenceau

When an American heiress wants to buy a man, she at once crosses the Atlantic. The only really materialistic people I have ever met are the Europeans.
Mary McCarthy

America is one long expectoration.
Oscar Wilde

It is absurd to say that there are neither ruins nor curiosities in America when they have their mothers and their manners.
Oscar Wilde

No one can be as calculatedly rude as the British, which amazes Americans, who do not understand studied insult and can only offer abuse as a substitute.
Paul Gallico

The United States, I believe, are under the impression that they are twenty years in advance of this country; whilst, as a matter of actual verifiable fact, of course, they are just about six hours behind it.
Harold Hobson, *The Devil in Woodford Wells*

The trouble with America is that there are far too many wide open spaces surrounded by teeth.
Charles Luckman

They have wonderful minds. So much is stored inside – all those sports scores and so on.
Jane Seymour on American men, in *Time*

America is a large, friendly dog in a very small room. Every time it wags its tail it knocks over a chair.
Arnold Toynbee

Americans are people who laugh at African witch doctors and spend 100 million dollars on fake reducing systems.
L. L. Levinson

To Americans English manners are far more frightening than none at all.
Randall Jarrell

The American male doesn't mature until he has exhausted all other possibilities.
Wilfred Sheed, *Office Politics*

The national dish of America is menus.
Robert Robinson

Show me a nation whose national beverage is beer, and I'll show you an advanced toilet technology.
Paul Hawkins

There won't be any revolution in America ... the people are too clean. They spend all their time changing their shirts and washing themselves. You can't feel fierce and revolutionary in a bathroom.
Eric Linklater, *Juan in America*

There is nothing the matter with Americans except their ideals. The real American is all right; it is the ideal American who is all wrong.
G. K. Chesterton

Knavery seems to be so much the striking feature of its inhabitants that it may not in the end be an evil that they will become aliens to this country.
George III on Americans

Paralytic sycophants, effete betrayers of humanity, carrion-eating servile imitators, arch-cowards and collaborators, gang of women-murderers, degenerate rabble, parasitic traditionalists, playboy soldiers, conceited dandies.

Approved terms of abuse in 1953 for East German Communist speakers when describing Britain

It is related of an Englishman that he hanged himself to avoid the daily task of dressing and undressing.

Johann Wolfgang von Goethe

The English think soap is civilization.

Heinrich von Treitschke

I know why the sun never sets on the British Empire: God wouldn't trust an Englishman in the dark.

Duncan Spaeth

Like a prostitute who, having sold her body all her life, decides to quit and close her business, and then tells everybody she wants to be chaste and protect her flesh as if it were jade.

He Manzi on Great Britain, in the Shanghai *Liberation Daily*. The reference is to Britain's discovery of a passion for democracy in Hong Kong under Chinese rule, having long denied Hong Kong democracy under British rule.

I wish I could bring Stonehenge to Nyasaland to show there was a time when Britain had a savage culture.

Dr Hastings Banda, President of Malawi, in the *Observer*

A demon took a monkey to wife – the result by the Grace of God was the English.

Indian saying

The departure of the Wise Men from the East seems to have been on a more extensive scale than is generally supposed, for no one of that description seems to have been left behind.
Sydney Smith on the East

Our trouble is that we drink too much tea. I see in this the slow revenge of the Orient, which has diverted the Yellow River down our throats.
J. B. Priestley

Taffy was a Welshman,
    Taffy was a thief,
Taffy came to my house
    And stole a piece of beef.

I went to Taffy's house,
    Taffy wasn't in,
I jumped upon his Sunday hat
    And poked it with a pin.

Taffy was a Welshman,
    Taffy was a sham,
Taffy came to my house
    And stole a leg of lamb.

I went to Taffy's house,
    Taffy was not there,
I hung his coat and trousers
    To roast before a fire.

Taffy was a Welshman,
    Taffy was a cheat,
Taffy came to my house
    And stole a piece of meat.

I went to Taffy's house,
    Taffy wasn't home;
Taffy came to my house
    And stole a marrow bone.
English nursery rhyme

A Welshman is a man who prays on his knees on Sunday and
preys on his friends the rest of the week.
Insult, probably of English origin

. . . an impotent people,
Sick with inbreeding,
Worrying the carcase of an old song.
R. S. Thomas, Welsh poet and clergyman, *An Acre of Land*, 'Welsh Landscape'

The land of my fathers. My fathers can have it.
Dylan Thomas on Wales

There are still parts of Wales where the only concession to
gaiety is a striped shroud.
Gwyn Thomas

The Welsh are so damn Welsh that it looks like affectation.
Sir Walter Alexander Raleigh to D. B. Wyndham Lewis

Other people have a nationality. The Irish and the Jews have
a psychosis.
Brendan Behan

Put an Irishman on the spit and you can always get another
Irishman to turn him.
George Bernard Shaw

I return your seasonal greetings card with contempt. May your hypocritical words choke you and may they choke you early in the New Year, rather than later.

Professor Kennedy Lindsay, a Vanguard member of the Northern Assembly, returning a Christmas card from the Minister for Foreign Affairs, Dr Garret FitzGerald, in the *Irish Times*

Ireland is the old sow that eats her farrow.

James Joyce, *A Portrait of the Artist as a Young Man*

The problem with Ireland is that it's a country full of genius, but with absolutely no talent.

Hugh Leonard, interview

An Irish queer is a fellow who prefers women to drink.

Sean O'Faolain

The moment the very name of Ireland is mentioned, the English seem to bid adieu to common feeling, common prudence, and common sense, and to act with the barbarity of tyrants, and the fatuity of idiots.

Sydney Smith

But of all nations in the world the English are perhaps the least a nation of pure philosophers.

Walter Bagehot

. . . where the Greeks had modesty, we have cant; where they had poetry, we have cant; where they had patriotism, we have cant; where they had anything that exalts, delights, or adorns humanity, we have nothing but cant, cant, cant.

Thomas Love Peacock, *Crotchet Castle*

A ready means of being cherished by the English is to adopt

the simple expedient of living a long time. I have little doubt that if, say, Oscar Wilde had lived into his nineties, instead of dying in his forties, he would have been considered a benign, distinguished figure suitable to preside at a school prize-giving or to instruct and exhort scoutmasters at their jamborees. He might even have been knighted.

Malcolm Muggeridge

The English people on the whole are surely the *nicest* people in the world, and everyone makes everything so easy for everybody else, that there is almost nothing to resist at all.

D. H. Lawrence, 'Dull London'

The English have an extraordinary ability for flying into a great calm.

Alexander Woollcott

Thirty millions, mostly fools.

Thomas Carlyle, when asked what the population of England was. Attrib.

I speak Spanish to God, Italian to women, French to men, and German to my horse.

Charles V, Holy Roman Emperor. Attrib.

Life is too short to learn German.

Richard Porson

German is a language which was developed solely to afford the speaker the opportunity to spit at strangers under the guise of polite conversation.

National Lampoon

The devil take these people and their language! They take a

dozen monosyllabic words in their jaws, chew them, crunch them and spit them out again, and call that speaking. Fortunately they are by nature fairly silent, and although they gaze at us open-mouthed, they spare us long conversations.
Heinrich Heine on the English

From every Englishman emanates a kind of gas, the deadly choke-damp of boredom.
Heinrich Heine

Unmitigated noodles.
Kaiser Wilhelm II of Germany on the English

How much disgruntled heaviness, lameness, dampness, dressing gown – how much *beer* there is in the German intelligence.
Friedrich Nietzsche, *Twilight of the Idols*

The English take their pleasures sadly, after the fashion of their country.
Maximilien de Béthune, Duc de Sully

The English are the people of consummate cant.
Friedrich Nietzsche, *Twilight of the Idols*

A family with the wrong members in control – that, perhaps, is as near as one can come to describing England in a phrase.
George Orwell, *The Lion and the Unicorn*, 'The Ruling Class'

England has become a squalid, uncomfortable, ugly place ... an intolerant, racist, homophobic, narrow-minded, authoritarian rat-hole run by vicious suburban-minded, materialistic philistines.
Hanif Kureishi, 1988

In Italy for thirty years under the Borgias they had warfare, terror, murder, bloodshed – they produced Michelangelo, Leonardo da Vinci and the Renaissance. In Switzerland they had brotherly love, five hundred years of democracy and peace, and what did they produce . . . ? The cuckoo clock.
Orson Welles, *The Third Man*

Since both its national products, snow and chocolate, melt, the cuckoo clock was invented solely in order to give tourists something solid to remember it by.
Alan Coren on Switzerland

I look upon Switzerland as an inferior sort of Scotland.
Sydney Smith

Oats. A grain, which in England is generally given to horses, but in Scotland supports the people.
Samuel Johnson, *Dictionary of the English Language*

It requires a surgical operation to get a joke well into a Scotch understanding.
Sydney Smith

Norway, too, has noble wild prospects; and Lapland is remarkable for prodigious noble wild prospects. But, Sir, let me tell you, the noblest prospect which a Scotchman ever sees, is the high road that leads him to England.
Samuel Johnson, *A Journey to the Western Islands of Scotland*

I have been trying all my life to like Scotchmen, and am obligated to desist from the experiment in despair.
Charles Lamb

The Scotchman is one who keeps the Sabbath and every other thing he can lay his hands on.
American insult

You've forgotten the grandest moral attribute of a Scotsman, Maggie, that he'll do nothing which might damage his career.
J. M. Barrie, *What Every Woman Knows*

DR JOHNSON: Sir, it is a very vile country.
MR S: Well, sir, God made it.
DR JOHNSON: Certainly he did, but we must remember that He made it for Scotchmen.
Samuel Johnson, *A Journey to the Western Islands of Scotland*

So you're going to Australia! . . . What are you going to sing? All I can say is – sing 'em muck! It's all they can understand!
Dame Nellie Melba, Australian soprano, speaking to Clara Butt

Pass a law to give every single whingeing bloody Pommie his fare home to England. Back to the smoke and the sun shining ten days a year and shit in the streets. Yer can have it.
Thomas Keneally, *The Chant of Jimmie Blacksmith*

I find it hard to say, because when I was there it seemed to be shut.
Clement Freud on being asked his opinion of New Zealand

Frustrate a Frenchman, he will drink himself to death; an Irishman, he will die of angry hypertension; a Dane, he will shoot himself; an American, he will get drunk, shoot you, then establish a million dollar aid programme for your relatives. Then he will die of an ulcer.
Stanley Rudin

Of course, America had often been discovered before Columbus, but it had always been hushed up.
Oscar Wilde

Poor Mexico, so far from God and so near to the United States!
Porfirio Díaz

Canada is useful only to provide me with furs.
Madame de Pompadour after the fall of Quebec

I don't even know what street Canada is on.
Al Capone

The people of Crete unfortunately make more history than they can consume locally.
Andrei Dimitrievich Sakharov

Bolivians are merely metamorphosed llamas who have learned to talk but not think.
Chilean Admiral José Toribio Merino

God made serpents and rabbits and Armenians.
Turkish insult

Do not trust a Hungarian unless he has a third eye in his forehead.
Czech insult

Half an Italian is one too many in a house.
German and French insult

Apart from cheese and tulips, the main product of Holland is advocaat, a drink made from lawyers.
Alan Coren, *The Sanity Inspector*

There are few virtues which the Poles do not possess and there are few errors they have ever avoided.
Winston Churchill

Beer is the Danish national drink and the Danish national weakness is another beer.
Clementine Paddleford

The Greeks – dirty and impoverished descendants of a bunch of la-de-da fruit salads who invented democracy and then forgot how to use it while walking around dressed up like girls.
P. J. O'Rourke, in the *National Lampoon*

Realizing that they will never be a world power, the Cypriots have decided to settle for being a world nuisance.
George Mikes

The indigested vomit of the sea
Fell to the Dutch by just propriety.
Andrew Marvell, 'The Character of Holland'

A nation is a society united by a delusion about its ancestry and by a common hatred of its neighbours.
William Ralph Inge, *A Perpetual Pessimist*

If I had to choose between betraying my country and betraying my friend, I hope I should have the guts to betray my country.
E. M. Forster, *Two Cheers for Democracy*, 'What I Believe'

Patriotism is the last refuge of the scoundrel.
Samuel Johnson

You gotta live somewhere.
Jimmy Brogan, a suggested motto for Cleveland, USA

They say that men become attached even to Widnes.
A. J. P. Taylor, in the *Observer*

Come, friendly bombs, and fall on Slough
It isn't fit for humans now.

. . .

Come, friendly bombs, and fall on Slough
To get it ready for the plough.
The cabbages are coming now;
    The earth exhales.
John Betjeman, *Continual Dew*, 'Slough'

One has no great hopes from Birmingham. I always say there
is something direful in the sound.
Jane Austen, *Emma*

They will steal the very teeth out of your mouth as you walk
the streets. I know it from experience.
Judge William Arabin, referring to the people of Uxbridge

New York . . . that unnatural city where everyone is an exile,
none more so than the American.
Charlotte Perkins Gilman

London, that great cesspool into which all the loungers of the
Empire are irresistibly drained.
Sir Arthur Conan Doyle, *A Study in Scarlet*

Rome's just a city like anywhere else. A vastly overrated city,
I'd say. It trades on belief just as Stratford trades on Shakespeare.
Anthony Burgess, *Inside Mr Enderby*

The river Rhine, it is well known,
Doth wash your city of Cologne;

But tell me, Nymphs, what power divine
Shall henceforth wash the river Rhine?
Samuel Taylor Coleridge, 'Cologne'

The young Cambridge group, the group that stood for 'freedom' and flannel trousers and flannel shirts open at the neck,
and a well-bred sort of emotional anarchy, and a whispering,
murmuring sort of voice, and an ultra-sensitive sort of manner.
D. H. Lawrence, *Lady Chatterley's Lover*

You will hear more good things on the outside of a stagecoach
from London to Oxford than if you were to pass a twelve-
month with the undergraduates, or heads of colleges, of that
famous university.
William Hazlitt, 'The Ignorance of the Learned'

Oxford is on the whole more attractive than Cambridge to the
ordinary visitor; and the traveller is therefore recommended to
visit Cambridge first, or to omit it altogether if he cannot visit
both.
Baedeker's Great Britain

Bugger Bognor.
George V, alleged last words when told by his doctor that he would soon be
well enough to visit Bognor Regis; also claimed as the king's response to the
proposal to rename the town Bognor Regis in honour of its recuperative
effect on His Majesty

Very flat, Norfolk.
Noël Coward, *Private Lives*

Shake a bridle over a Yorkshireman's grave and he will rise
and steal a horse.
Lancashire saying

California is a place in which a boom mentality and a sense of Chekhovian loss meet in uneasy suspension.
Joan Didion

Great God! this is an awful place.
Captain Robert Falcon Scott on the South Pole

Bastards sitting in their offices
And bastards trying to boss you around
Bastards up there in Canberra
You expect those bastards to be bastards
    But what gets me
Is having bastards all around you
Bastards on your own side who turn out to be
Bastards.
I guarantee if they started a society
To rid the world of bastards
In six months the bastards
Would take it over.
Len Fox, *Gumleaves and People*

There exists no politician in India daring enough to attempt to explain to the masses that cows can be eaten.
Indira Gandhi

It is by the goodness of God that in our country we have those three unspeakably precious things: freedom of speech, freedom of conscience, and the prudence never to practise either of them.
Mark Twain

Have I said something foolish?
Athenian statesman to colleague, on being cheered by the crowd

Democracy means government by discussion but it is only effective if you can stop people talking.
Clement Attlee

Too bad all the people who know how to run the country are busy driving cabs and cutting hair.
George Burns

One fifth of the people are against everything all the time.
Robert Kennedy

Only constant repetition will finally succeed in imprinting an idea on the memory of the crowd.
Adolf Hitler, *Mein Kampf*

Would that the Roman people had one neck!
Caligula

The public buys its opinions as it buys its meat, or takes in its milk, on the principle that it is cheaper to do this than to keep a cow.
Samuel Butler

That garrulous monk.
Benito Mussolini on Adolf Hitler

The broad mass of a nation ... will more easily fall victim to a big lie than to a small one.
Adolf Hitler, *Mein Kampf*

Well, you might try getting crucified and rising again on the third day.
Talleyrand on what might impress the French peasantry

You cannot make a man by standing a sheep on its hind legs.
But by standing a flock of sheep in that position you can make
a crowd of men.
Max Beerbohm, *Zuleika Dobson*

What men call social virtues, good fellowship, is commonly
but the virtue of pigs in a litter, which lie in close together to
keep each other warm.
Henry David Thoreau

The people would be just as noisy if they were going to see
me hanged.
Oliver Cromwell, referring to a noisy crowd of admirers

Out of the crooked timber of humanity no straight thing can
ever be made.
Immanuel Kant, *Idee zu einer allgemeinen Geschichte in weltbürgerlicher Absicht*

There is something utterly nauseating about a system of society
which pays a harlot 25 times as much as it pays its Prime
Minister, 250 times as much as it pays its Members of Parliament, and 500 times as much as it pays some of its ministers
of religion.
Harold Wilson on the case of Christine Keeler

From Lord Hailsham we have had a virtuoso performance in
the art of kicking a friend in the guts. When self-indulgence
has reduced a man to the shape of Lord Hailsham, sexual
continence involves no more than a sense of the ridiculous.
Reginald Paget on Lord Hailsham, following the Profumo scandal

'What have you done?' cried Christine,
'You've wrecked the whole party machine!

'To lie in the nude
'May be rude,
'But to lie in the House is obscene!'
Anonymous, on John Profumo, about the Profumo scandal

Here lies our sovereign Lord the King,
Whose word no man relies on,
Who never said a foolish thing,
Nor ever did a wise one.
John Wilmot, Earl of Rochester, on Charles II

This is very true: for my words are my own, and my actions
are my ministers'.
Charles II

... a pig, an ass, a dunghill, the spawn of an adder, a basilisk,
a lying buffoon, a mad fool with a frothy mouth ... a lubberly
ass ... a frantic madman ...
Martin Luther on Henry VIII

Great Wits are sure to Madness near alli'd
And thin Partitions do their Bounds divide ...
John Dryden on the Earl of Shaftesbury, *Absalom and Achitophel*

His imagination resembled the wings of an ostrich. It enabled
him to run, though not to soar.
Thomas Babington Macaulay on John Dryden

A Cherub's face, a reptile all the rest;
Beauty that shocks you, parts that none will trust,
Wit that can creep, and pride that licks the dust.
Alexander Pope on Baron John Hervey, *An Epistle to Dr Arbuthnot*

He hardly drank tea without a stratagem.
Samuel Johnson on Alexander Pope

Damn with faint praise, assent with civil leer,
And without sneering, teach the rest to sneer;
Willing to wound, and yet afraid to strike,
Just hint a fault, and hesitate dislike;
Alike reserved to blame, or to commend,
A tim'rous foe, and a suspicious friend . . .
Alexander Pope on Joseph Addison, *An Epistle to Dr Arbuthnot*

His Grace! impossible! what dead!
Of old age too, and in his bed!
And could that Mighty Warrior fall?
And so inglorious, after all! . . .
   Come hither, all ye empty things,
Ye bubbles rais'd by breath of Kings;
Who float upon the tide of state,
Come hither, and behold your fate.
Let pride be taught by this rebuke,
How very mean a thing's a Duke;
From all his ill-got honours flung,
Turn'd to that dirt from whence he sprung.
Jonathan Swift on John Churchill, Duke of Marlborough, 'A Satirical Elegy
on the Death of a late Famous General'

Had it not been for the good nature of these very mortals
they contemn, these two superior beings were entitled, by
their birth and hereditary fortune, to be only a couple of link-
boys. I am of opinion their friendship would have continued,
though they had remained in the same kingdom: it had a very

strong foundation – the love of flattery on one side, and the love of money on the other.

Lady Mary Wortley Montagu on Jonathan Swift and Alexander Pope, letter to the Countess of Bute

My Dear Sir,

In times like the present, it is impossible to allow private feelings to take the place of a public sense of duty. I think your conduct as dangerous in Parliament as it is in your own county. Were you my own brother, therefore, I could not give you my support.

Thomas Liddell to J. G. Lambton, who was contesting the Durham constituency, letter

My Dear Sir Thomas,

In answer to your letter, I beg to say that I feel gratitude for your frankness, compassion for your fears, little dread of your opposition, and no want of your support.

J. G. Lambton to Thomas Liddell, in reply

Gentlemen,

I received yours and am surprised by your insolence in troubling me about the Excise. You know, what I very well know, that I bought you. And I know, what perhaps you think I don't know, you are now selling yourselves to Somebody Else; and I know, what you do not know, that I am buying another borough. May God's curse light upon you all: may your houses be as open and common to all Excise Officers as your wives and daughters were to me, when I stood for your scoundrel corporation.

Yours, etc., Anthony Henley

Letter from Anthony Henley, MP for Southampton (1727–34), to his constituents, following their protests over the Excise Bill

The Right Honourable gentleman is indebted to his memory for his jests, and to his imagination for his facts.
Richard Brinsley Sheridan, replying to a speech in the House of Commons by Henry Dundas. Attrib.

Mr Speaker, I said the honourable member was a liar it is true and I am sorry for it. The honourable member may place the punctuation where he pleases.
Richard Brinsley Sheridan, on being asked to apologize for calling a fellow MP a liar. Attrib.

Lord Talbot's horse, like the great planet in Milton, danced about in various rounds his wandering course. At different times, he was progressive, retrograde, or standing still. The progressive motion I should rather incline to think the merit of the horse, the retrograde motion, the merit of the Lord.
John Wilkes on the conduct of the Earl of Talbot's horse at the coronation of George III, *The North Briton*, 1762

Therefore I charge Mr Hastings with having destroyed, for private purposes, the whole system of government by the six provincial Councils, which he had no right to destroy.
 I charge him with taking bribes of Gunga Govind Sing.
 I charge him with not having done that bribe-service which fidelity, even in iniquity, requires at the hands of the worst of men.
 I charge him with having robbed those persons of whom he took the bribes.

I charge him with having fraudulently alienated the fortunes of widows.

I charge him with having, without right, title or purchase, taken the lands of orphans and given them to wicked persons under him.

I charge him with having removed the natural guardians of a minor Raja, and given his zamindary to that wicked person, Deby Sing.

I charge him – his wickedness being known to himself and all the world – with having committed to Deby Sing the management of three great provinces; and with having thereby wasted the country, destroyed the landed interest, cruelly harassed the peasants, burnt their houses, seized their crops, tortured and degraded their persons, and destroyed the honour of the whole female race of that country.

Edmund Burke, peroration on Warren Hastings, 1788

Burke was a damned wrong-headed fellow, through his whole life jealous and obstinate.

Charles James Fox on Edmund Burke. Attrib.

... two vultures sick for battle,
  Two scorpions under one wet stone,
Two bloodless wolves whose dry throats rattle,
Two crows perched on the murrained cattle,
    Two vipers tangled into one.

Percy Bysshe Shelley, 'Similes for two political characters of 1819' – the Home Secretary Sidmouth, and Foreign Secretary and Leader of the Commons Castlereagh

Why is a pump like Viscount Castlereagh? –

Because it is a slender thing of wood,
That up and down its awkward arm doth sway,
And coolly spout and spout and spout away,
In one weak, washy, everlasting flood.
Thomas Moore on Viscount Castlereagh

I met Murder on the way –
He had a mask like Castlereagh...
Percy Bysshe Shelley, *The Mask of Anarchy*

The Right Honourable Gentleman's smile is like the silver
fittings on a coffin.
Benjamin Disraeli on Sir Robert Peel

You owe the Whigs a great gratitude, my Lord, and therefore
I think you will betray them. For your Lordship is like a
favourite footman on easy terms with his mistress. Your dex-
terity seems a happy compound of the smartness of an
attorney's clerk and the intrigue of a Greek of the lower
empire.
Benjamin Disraeli on Lord Palmerston

If a traveller were informed that such a man was the Leader
of the House of Commons, he might begin to comprehend
how the Egyptians worshipped an insect.
Benjamin Disraeli on Lord John Russell

... a systematic liar and a beggarly cheat; a swindler and a
poltroon ... He has committed every crime that does not
require courage.
Benjamin Disraeli on the Irish agitator Daniel O'Connell

He is a liar. (Cheers) He is a liar in action and in words. His life is a living lie. He is a disgrace to his species. What state of society must be that could tolerate such a creature – having the audacity to come forward with one set of principles at one time, and obtain political assistance by reason of those principles, and at another to profess diametrically the reverse? His life, I say again, is a living lie. He is the most degraded of his species and kind; and England is degraded in tolerating or having upon the face of her society a miscreant of his abominable, foul and atrocious nature. (Cheers) ... It will not be supposed ... when I speak to D'Israeli as the descendant of a Jew, that I mean to tarnish him on that account. They were once the chosen people of God. There were miscreants amongst them however, also, and it must certainly have been from one of these that D'Israeli descended. (Roars of laughter) He possesses just the qualities of the impenitent thief who died upon the Cross, whose name, I verily believe, must have been D'Israeli. (Roars of laughter) For aught I know, the present D'Israeli is descended from him, and, with the impression that he is, I now forgive the heir-at-law of the blasphemous thief who died upon the Cross. (Loud cheers and roars of laughter)

Daniel O'Connell on Benjamin Disraeli, at a meeting of trades unions in Dublin

London, May 6 [1835]

Mr O'Connell:

Although you have long placed yourself out of the pale of civilization, still I am one who will not be insulted, even by a Yahoo, without chastising it ... Listen, then, to me.

If it had been possible for you to act like a gentleman, you would have hesitated before you made your foul and insolent comments . . . I admire your scurrilous allusions to my origin. It is quite clear that the 'hereditary bondman' has already forgotten the clank of his fetter . . . With regard to your taunts as to my want of success in my election contests, permit me to remind you that I had nothing to appeal to but the good sense of the people . . . My pecuniary resources, too, were limited; I am not one of those public beggars that we see swarming with their obtrusive boxes in the chapels of your creed, nor am I in possession of a princely revenue wrung from a starving race of fanatical slaves . . .

We shall meet at Philippi; and . . . I will seize the first opportunity of inflicting upon you a castigation which will make you at the same time remember and repent the insults you have lavished upon

BENJAMIN DISRAELI

Benjamin Disraeli to Daniel O'Connell

As I sat opposite the Treasury Bench, the Ministers reminded me of one of those marine landscapes not very unusual on the coasts of South America. You behold a range of exhausted volcanoes, not a flame flickers on a single pallid crest, but the situation is still dangerous. There are occasional earthquakes, and ever and anon the dark rumbling of the sea.

Benjamin Disraeli on the Liberal Government

There is not a criminal in an European gaol, there is not a cannibal in the South Sea Islands, whose indignation would not rise and boil at the recital of that which has been done, which has too late been examined, but which remains

unavenged; which has left behind all the foul and all the fierce passions that produced it, and which may again spring up, in another murderous harvest, from the soil soaked and reeking in blood, and in the air tainted with every imaginable deed of crime and shame. That such things should be done once, is a damning disgrace to the portion of our race which did them; that a door should be left open for their ever-so-barely possible repetition would spread that shame over the whole . . .
W. E. Gladstone on the Turks, *Bulgarian Horrors and the Question of the East*

He made his conscience not his guide but his accomplice.
Benjamin Disraeli on W. E. Gladstone

He has not a single redeeming defect.
Benjamin Disraeli on W. E. Gladstone

If Gladstone fell into the Thames, that would be a misfortune, and if anybody pulled him out that, I suppose, would be a calamity.
Benjamin Disraeli on W. E. Gladstone, after being asked to distinguish a misfortune and a calamity

He was without any rival whatever, the first comic genius who ever installed himself in Downing Street.
Michael Foot on Benjamin Disraeli

A sophistical rhetorician, inebriated with the exuberance of his own verbosity, and gifted with an egotistical imagination, that can at all times command an interminable and inconsistent series of arguments, malign an opponent and glorify himself.
Benjamin Disraeli on W. E. Gladstone, parodying his style

Mr Gladstone speaks to me as if I were a public meeting.
Queen Victoria on W. E. Gladstone

... an old, wild, and incomprehensible man ...
Queen Victoria on W. E. Gladstone's fourth and last appointment as Prime
Minister

Cannes, March 15, 1893
Far away from my native Land, my bitter indignation as a
Welshwoman prompts me to reproach you, you bad, wicked,
false, treacherous Old Man! ... You have no conscience, but
I pray that God may even yet give you one that will sorely
smart and trouble you before you die. You pretend to be
religious, you old hypocrite! that you may more successfully
pander to the evil passions of the lowest and most ignorant of
the Welsh people ... You think you will shine in history, but
it will be a notoriety similar to that of Nero. I see someone
pays you the unintentional compliment of comparing you to
Pontius Pilate, and I am sorry, for Pilate, though a political
time-server, was, with all his faults, a very respectable man in
comparison with you ... You are certainly cleverer. So also is
your lord and master the Devil. And I cannot regard it as
sinful to hate and despise you, any more than it is sinful to
abhor Him. So with full measure of contempt and detestation,
accept these compliments from
'A DAUGHTER OF OLD WALES'
Anonymous letter to W. E. Gladstone, following his proposals to change the
Welsh church

The ordinary women of Wales are generally short and squat,
ill-favoured and nasty.
David Mallet to Alexander Pope

If you weren't such a great man you'd be a terrible bore.
Mrs W. E. Gladstone to her husband

Mr Gladstone read Homer for fun, which I thought served him right.
Winston Churchill on W. E. Gladstone

All the faults of the age come from Christianity and Journalism.
Frank Harris

Christianity, of course, but why journalism?
Arthur James Balfour in reply

I hesitate to say what the functions of the modern journalist may be, but I imagine that they do not exclude the intelligent anticipation of facts before they occur.
Lord Curzon

The government of bullies, tempered by editors.
Ralph Waldo Emerson on democracy

What the proprietorship of these papers is aiming at is power, and power without responsibility – the prerogative of the harlot throughout the ages.
Stanley Baldwin on the press barons Lords Rothermere and Beaverbrook

Good God, that's done it. He's lost us the tarts' vote.
The 10th Duke of Devonshire on Stanley Baldwin's attack on newspaper proprietors. Attrib.

Politicians who complain about the media are like ships' captains who complain about the sea.
Enoch Powell

I am dead: dead, but in the Elysian fields.
Benjamin Disraeli on his move to the House of Lords. Attrib.

This is a rotten argument, but it should be good enough for
their lordships on a hot summer afternoon.
Anonymous note on a ministerial brief read out by mistake in the House of
Lords, quoted in *The Way the Wind Blows* by Lord Home

It is very easy, my Lord, to swing about in the House of Lords,
and to be brave five years after the time, and to point out to
their Lordships the clear difference between moral and physical fear, and to be nodded to by the Duke of Wellington, but
I am not to be paid by such coin.
Sydney Smith, letter to *The Times*, attacking the Bishop of London, Charles
James Blomfield, for his support of the Ecclesiastical Commission of 1836

I made his honour my most humble acknowledgements for
the good opinion he was pleased to conceive of me; but
assured him, at the same time, that my birth was of the lower
sort, having been born of plain honest parents, who were just
able to give me a tolerable education; that nobility among us
was altogether a different thing from the idea he had of it; that
our young noblemen are bred from their childhood in idleness
and luxury; that as soon as years will permit, they consume
their vigour, and contract odious diseases, among lewd
females; and when their fortunes are almost ruined, they
marry some woman of mean birth, disagreeable person, and
unsound constitution, merely for the sake of money, whom
they hate and despise; that the productions of such marriages
are generally scrofulous, rickety, or deformed children; by
which means the family seldom continues above three gen-

erations, unless the wife takes care to provide a healthy father, among her neighbours or domestics, in order to improve and continue the breed; that a weak, diseased body, a meagre countenance, and sallow complexion, are the true marks of noble blood; and a healthy, robust appearance is so disgraceful in a man of quality, that the world concludes his real father to have been a groom or coachman. The imperfections of his mind run parallel with those of his body, being a composition of spleen, dulness, ignorance, caprice, sensuality, and pride.

Without the consent of this illustrious body no law can be enacted, repealed, or altered; and these nobles have likewise the decision of all our possessions, without appeal.

Jonathan Swift, *Gulliver's Travels*. Gulliver on the English nobility

A fully equipped Duke costs as much to keep up as two Dreadnoughts, and Dukes are just as great a terror, and they last longer.

David Lloyd George

The House of Lords is like a glass of champagne that has stood for five days.

Clement Attlee. Attrib.

Every man has a House of Lords in his own head. Fears, prejudices, misconceptions – those are the peers, and they are hereditary.

David Lloyd George

An ermine-lined dustbin, an up-market geriatric home with a faint smell of urine.

Austin Mitchell on the House of Lords

What shall we do with this bauble? There, take it away.
Oliver Cromwell, speech dismissing Parliament

Let me be thankful, God, that I am not
A Labour Leader when his life-work ends,
Who contemplates the coronet he got
By being false to principles and friends;

Who fought for forty years a desperate fight
With words that seared and stung and slew like swords,
And at the end, with victory in sight,
Ate them – a mushroom viscount in the Lords.
William Kean Seymour, 'Viscount Demos'

He occasionally stumbled over the truth, but hastily picked
himself up and hurried on as if nothing had happened.
Winston Churchill on Stanley Baldwin

Like a cushion, he always bore the impress of the last man
who sat on him.
David Lloyd George on Lord Derby; also attrib. to Lord Haig

The two most powerful men in Russia are Tsar Nicholas II
and the last person who spoke to him.
Anonymous

This goat-footed bard, this half-human visitor to our age
from the hag-ridden magic and enchanted woods of Celtic
antiquity.
John Maynard Keynes on David Lloyd George, *Essays and Sketches in Biography*,
1933

The tenth possessor of a foolish face.
David Lloyd George on any aristocrat

When they circumcised Herbert Samuel they threw away the wrong bit.
David Lloyd George. Attrib. in the *Listener*, 1978

He could not see a belt without hitting below it.
Margot Asquith on David Lloyd George

The Right Honourable gentleman has sat so long on the fence that the iron has entered his soul.
David Lloyd George on Sir John Simon. Attrib.

The Right Honourable and Learned Gentleman has twice crossed the floor of this House, each time leaving behind a trail of slime.
David Lloyd George on Sir John Simon

My one ardent desire is that after the war he should be publicly castrated in front of Nurse Cavell's statue.
Lytton Strachey on David Lloyd George

It is fitting that we should have buried the Unknown Prime Minister by the side of the Unknown Soldier.
Herbert Asquith at Andrew Bonar Law's funeral. Attrib.

If I am a great man, then a good many of the great men of history are frauds.
Andrew Bonar Law. Attrib.

I must follow them; I am their leader.
Andrew Bonar Law

I met Curzon in Downing Street, from whom I got the sort of greeting a corpse would give to an undertaker.
Stanley Baldwin. Attrib.

One could not even dignify him with the name of a stuffed shirt. He was simply a hole in the air.
George Orwell on Stanley Baldwin

I think Baldwin has gone mad. He simply takes one jump in the dark; looks around and then takes another.
Lord Birkenhead on Stanley Baldwin

I would rather be an opportunist and float, than go to the bottom with my principles round my neck.
Stanley Baldwin

Decided only to be undecided, resolved to be irresolute, adamant for drift, solid for fluidity, all-powerful to be impotent.
Winston Churchill on Stanley Baldwin

He saw foreign policy through the wrong end of a municipal drainpipe.
Winston Churchill on Neville Chamberlain; also attrib. to David Lloyd George

You have sat too long here for any good you have been doing. Depart, I say, and let us have done with you. In the name of God, *go*!
Leopold Amery to Neville Chamberlain, using Cromwell's words

He is no better than a Mayor of Birmingham, and in a lean year at that. Furthermore he is too old. He thinks he understands the modern world. What should an old hunk like him know of the modern world?
Lord Hugh Cecil on Neville Chamberlain

He has the lucidity which is the by-product of a fundamentally sterile mind ... Listening to a speech by Chamberlain is like paying a visit to Woolworth's; everything in its place and nothing above sixpence.
Aneurin Bevan on Neville Chamberlain

The people of Birmingham have a specially heavy burden for they have given the world the curse of the present British Prime Minister.
Sir Stafford Cripps on Neville Chamberlain

There but for the grace of God goes God.
Winston Churchill on Sir Stafford Cripps

Wherever Stafford has tried to increase the sum of human happiness, grass never grows again.
Anonymous, on Sir Stafford Cripps

Well, he seemed such a nice old gentleman, I thought I would give him my autograph as a souvenir.
Adolf Hitler on Neville Chamberlain

He was a meticulous housemaid, great at tidying up.
A. J. P. Taylor on Neville Chamberlain

I remember, when I was a child, being taken to the celebrated Barnum's Circus, which contained an exhibition of freaks and monstrosities; but the exhibit on the programme which I most desired to see was the one described 'The Boneless Wonder'. My parents judged that that spectacle would be too revolting and demoralizing for my youthful eyes, and I have waited fifty years to see The Boneless Wonder sitting on the Treasury Bench.

Winston Churchill on Ramsay MacDonald

Winston had devoted the best years of his life to preparing his impromptu speeches.

F. E. Smith on Winston Churchill

He is one of those orators of whom it was well said, 'Before they get up they do not know what they are going to say; when they are speaking, they do not know what they are saying; and when they sit down, they do not know what they have said.'

Winston Churchill on Charles Beresford

Begotten of froth out of foam.

Herbert Asquith on Winston Churchill

Tell the Lord Privy Seal I am sealed to my privy, and can only deal with one shit at a time.

Winston Churchill when interrupted on the toilet in his wartime bunker and told the Lord Privy Seal wished to see him. Attrib.

WANTED! Dead or alive! Winston Churchill. 25 years old. 5 feet 8 inches tall. Indifferent build. Walks with a bend forward. Pale complexion. Red-brownish hair. Small toothbrush moustache. Talks through his nose and cannot pronounce the letter 'S' properly.

Jan Smuts on Winston Churchill

I thought he was a young man of promise; but it appears he was a young man of promises.

Arthur James Balfour, writing in his diary of Winston Churchill's entry into politics

A glass of port in his hand and a fat cigar in his mouth, with a huge and bloody red steak which he puts in his mouth in big chunks, and chews and chatters and mokes until the blood trickles down his chin – and to think this monster comes of a good family.

Joseph Goebbels on Winston Churchill

A sheep in sheep's clothing.

Winston Churchill on Clement Attlee

He is a man suffering from petrified adolescence.

Aneurin Bevan on Winston Churchill

A tardy little marionette.

Randolph Churchill on Clement Attlee, in the *Evening Standard*

A triumph of modern science – to find the only part of Randolph that wasn't malignant and remove it.

Evelyn Waugh on Randolph Churchill after an operation

An empty taxi arrived at 10 Downing Street, and when the door was opened Attlee got out.

Winston Churchill (attrib.) on Clement Attlee. But Kenneth Harris (*Attlee*, 1982) says Churchill denied the quote: 'Mr Attlee is an honourable and gallant gentleman, and a faithful colleague who has served his country well at the time of her greatest need. I should be obliged if you would make it clear whenever an occasion arises that I would never make such a remark about him and I strongly disapprove of anyone who does.'

I welcome this opportunity of pricking the bloated bladder of lies with the poniard of truth.
Aneurin Bevan on Winston Churchill

He will be as great a curse to this country in peace as he was a squalid nuisance in time of war.
Winston Churchill on Aneurin Bevan

Christopher, I don't think Mr Mikardo is such a nice man as he looks.
Winston Churchill to his PPS, Christopher Soames, about Ian Mikardo, who was a famously ugly MP. Sir Edward Heath told us that this remark was made after a debate in the House of Commons in which Mr Mikardo 'pressed the Prime Minister about anti-Semitic practices at the Mid-Ocean Club, Bermuda, somewhat to the irritation of the Prime Minister'.

Always in the wrong, always surrounded by crooks, a most unsuccessful father – simply a 'Radio personality' who out-lived his prime.
Evelyn Waugh on Winston Churchill

A difficulty for every solution.
Herbert Samuel on the civil service

No amount of cajolery, and no attempts at ethical and social seduction, can eradicate from my heart a deep burning hatred for the Tory Party . . . So far as I am concerned they are lower than vermin.
Aneurin Bevan

An overripe banana, yellow outside, squishy in.
Sir Reginald Paget on Anthony Eden

He is not only a bore, but he bores for England.
Malcolm Muggeridge on Sir Anthony Eden

Muggeridge, a garden gnome expelled from Eden, has come to rest as a gargoyle brooding over a derelict cathedral.
Kenneth Tynan on Malcolm Muggeridge

I wonder if I might have a translation.
Harold Macmillan during an address to the UN Security Council after Nikita Khrushchev, seated opposite, disagreed so vehemently that he took off his shoe and banged the heel on the table

It was almost impossible to believe he was anything but a down-at-heel actor resting between engagements at the decrepit theatres of minor provincial towns.
Bernard Levin on Harold Macmillan, *The Pendulum Years*

Greater love hath no man than this, that he lay down his friends for his life.
Jeremy Thorpe after Harold Macmillan's 1962 Cabinet reshuffle

One can never escape the suspicion, with Mr Macmillan, that all his life was a preparation for elder statesmanship.
Frank Johnson on Harold Macmillan, in *The Times*

He is going around the country stirring up apathy.
William Whitelaw on Harold Wilson

If ever he went to school without any boots it was because he was too big for them.
Ivor Bulmer-Thomas on Harold Wilson

As far as the 14th Earl is concerned, I suppose Mr Wilson, when you come to think of it, is the 14th Mr Wilson.
Sir Alec Douglas-Home on renouncing his peerage as the 14th Earl of Home to become Prime Minister

SIR ALEC DOUGLAS-HOME: Tell me, Mr Chairman, what do you think would have happened if Mr Khrushchev had been assassinated and not President Kennedy?

CHAIRMAN MAO: I do not believe Mr Onassis would have married Mrs Khrushchev.

Exchange at an official dinner

The Minister of Technology flung himself into the Sixties technology with the enthusiasm (not to say the language) of a newly enrolled Boy Scout demonstrating knot-tying to his indulgent parents.

Bernard Levin on Tony Benn, *The Pendulum Years*

If I rescued a child from drowning, the press would no doubt headline the story 'Benn grabs child'.

Tony Benn

The Bertie Wooster of Marxism

Anonymous, about Tony Benn

A little boy sucking his misogynist thumb and blubbing and carping in the corner of the front bench below the gangway is a mascot which parliament can do without.

Nicholas Fairbairn on Edward Heath

A perfectly good second-class chemist, a Beta chemist ... she wasn't an interesting person, except as a Conservative ... I would never, if I had amusing, interesting people staying, have thought of asking Margaret Thatcher.

Dame Janet Vaughan (former tutor at Somerville College, Oxford) on Margaret Thatcher

Mrs Thatcher is a woman of common views but uncommon abilities.
Julian Critchley on Margaret Thatcher

... the powers of a first-rate man and the creed of a second-rate man.
Walter Bagehot on Sir Robert Peel

She is happier getting in and out of tanks than in and out of museums or theatre seats. She seems to derive more pleasure from admiring new missiles than great works of art. What else can we expect from an ex-Spam hoarder from Grantham presiding over the social and economic decline of the country?
Tony Banks on Margaret Thatcher

If she has a weakness it is for shopkeepers, which probably accounts for the fact that she cannot pass a branch of Marks and Spencers without inviting the manager to join her private office.
Julian Critchley on Margaret Thatcher

The Prime Minister tells us that she has given the French president a piece of her mind – not a gift I would receive with alacrity.
Denis Healey on Margaret Thatcher

I wouldn't say she is open-minded on the Middle East, so much as empty-headed. She probably thinks Sinai is the plural of Sinus.
Jonathan Aitken on Margaret Thatcher

She's a handbag economist who believes that you pay as you go.
New Yorker on Margaret Thatcher

She approaches the problems of our country with all the one-dimensional subtlety of a comic strip.
Denis Healey on Margaret Thatcher

La Pasionaria of middle-class privilege.
Denis Healey on Margaret Thatcher

Pétain in petticoats.
Denis Healey on Margaret Thatcher

Rhoda the Rhino.
Denis Healey on Margaret Thatcher

The great she-elephant.
Julian Critchley on Margaret Thatcher

Jezebel.
Revd Ian Paisley on Margaret Thatcher

The Immaculate Misconception.
Norman St John-Stevas on Margaret Thatcher

Attila the Hen.
Clement Freud on Margaret Thatcher

David Owen in drag.
Rhodesia Herald on Margaret Thatcher

One of the things that politics has taught me is that men are not a reasoned or reasonable sex.
Margaret Thatcher

It is said that at one of her weekly audiences with the Queen, the then Mrs Thatcher was dismayed that she and the Queen were wearing identical outfits. She asked her office to suggest to the Palace that, to avoid embarrassment, they inform her in advance of Her Majesty's proposed dress. 'That will not be necessary,' was the response. 'Her Majesty does not notice what other people are wearing.'

An often quoted story

I wasn't lucky. I deserved it.

Margaret Thatcher, aged nine, after receiving a school prize

On the last Sunday of the 1983 General Election campaign I represented the Labour Party at a 'Question Time' organized by TVS in Gillingham, Kent, and filmed before an audience. Whilst I was responding to a question about Margaret Thatcher, a member of the audience interrupted with a shout of 'At least she's got guts'. I responded immediately by saying 'It's a pity that others had to lose theirs at Goose Green to prove it.'

Neil Kinnock, letter to the editor of this book. Mr Kinnock points out that there were demands that he withdraw his statement. He didn't, he says, 'not least because several people in, or associated with, the Forces took the trouble to let me know that they thought I should stand by what I said'.

The self-appointed king of the gutter.

Michael Heseltine on Neil Kinnock after the above attack on Margaret Thatcher

If I was in the gutter, and I ain't, he'd still be looking up at me from the sewer.

Neil Kinnock on Michael Heseltine

He reminds me of a Scottish Buddha, the very essence of immobility with a faint smile of perfect self-contentment upon his face.

John Major on John Smith

John Major himself now veers towards the ridiculous, whether flourishing his meaningless Citizen's Charter, tinkering with the Honours List, litigating alongside his cook, half-attacking Margaret Thatcher in the *Independent* – then backing down in fear and confusion – bickering with his archbishops or giving two cheers (one, really) for his embattled Queen. Not a man to go tiger-shooting with, even if the brutes were drugged or indeed stuffed. If I saw the Captain with a gun I would head for cover . . .

. . . John Major, in my estimation, is not the man to frog-march his party towards what he conceives to be his destiny . . . Major is what he is: a man from nowhere, going nowhere, heading for a well-merited obscurity as fast as his mediocre talents can carry him . . .

Paul Johnson, in the *Spectator*, March 1993

John Major, Norman Lamont: I wouldn't spit in their mouths if their teeth were on fire.

Rodney Bickerstaffe of UNISON, 1992, who said this was based on a Scottish insult he learned in his youth: 'I wouldn't piss down his throat if his chest was on fire.'

How can one best summon up the exquisite, earnest tedium of the speech of Sir Geoffrey Howe in yesterday's South African debate? It was rather like watching a much-loved

family tortoise creeping over the lawn in search of a distant tomato.
David McKie on Sir Geoffrey Howe

Like being savaged by a dead sheep.
Denis Healey, referring to the attack by Sir Geoffrey Howe upon his Budget proposals, in the *Listener*

Like being flogged with a warm lettuce.
Australian Prime Minister Paul Keating, referring to an attack by the Opposition leader, John Hewson

The outstanding surviving example of English baroque.
Michael White on Norman St John-Stevas

A Conservative government is an organized hypocrisy.
Benjamin Disraeli

The Honourable Member for two tube stations.
Nicholas Fairbairn on Frank Dobson (MP for Holborn and St Pancras)

Like a fist fight in a hydrangea bush.
Craig Brown on Dame Jill Knight wearing a floral print

His delivery at the dispatch-box has all the bite of a rubber duck.
Marcia Lady Falkender on John Moore

Like Woody Allen without the jokes.
Simon Hoggart on Sir Keith Joseph

John Stuart Mill rewritten by Ernest Hemingway.
Chris Patten on David Owen

A desiccated calculating machine.
Aneurin Bevan, usually regarded as a jibe at Hugh Gaitskell

A feral calculator.
Paul Keating on John Hewson, 1993 Australian general election

They are nothing else but a load of kippers – two-faced, with
no guts.
Eric Heffer on the Conservative Government

A semi-house-trained polecat.
Michael Foot on Norman Tebbit

Far better to keep your mouth shut and let everyone think
you're stupid than to open it and leave no doubt.
Norman Tebbit to Dennis Skinner

The weak are a long time in politics.
Neil Shand on John Gummer

Drittsekk.
Thorbjørn Berntsen on John Gummer. British newspapers translated the
word as 'shitbag', but the Royal Norwegian Embassy suggests a better translation is 'twerp'.

He is undoubtedly living proof that a pig's bladder on a stick
can be elected as a member of parliament.
Tony Banks on fellow MP Terry Dicks

A political leader worthy of assassination.
Irving Layton on Pierre Trudeau

An improbable creature, like a human giraffe, sniffing down
his nostril at mortals beneath his gaze.
Richard Wilson on Charles de Gaulle

A horrible voice, bad breath and a vulgar manner – the characteristics of a popular politician.
Aristophanes

It is inexcusable for scientists to torture animals; let them make their experiments on journalists and politicians.
Henrik Ibsen

A politician is a statesman who approaches every question with an open mouth.
Adlai Stevenson

I know what a statesman is. He's a dead politician. We need more statesmen.
Robert C. Edwards. Attrib.

When a politician changes his position it's sometimes hard to tell whether he has seen the light or felt the heat.
Robert Fuoss

In our time, political speech and writing are largely the defence of the indefensible.
George Orwell, *Politics and the English Language*

Few things are as immutable as the addiction of political groups to the ideas by which they have once won office.
John Kenneth Galbraith, *The Affluent Society*

Since a politician never believes what he says, he is surprised when others believe him.
Charles de Gaulle. Attrib.

In politics there is no honour.
Benjamin Disraeli

The reason there are so few female politicians is that it is too much trouble to put make-up on two faces.
Maureen Murphy

It is now known ... that men enter local politics solely as a result of being unhappily married.
Cyril Northcote Parkinson

Politics, as a practice, whatever its professions, had always been the systematic organization of hatred.
Henry Adams, *The Education of Henry Adams*

Politicians can forgive almost anything in the way of abuse; they can forgive subversion, revolution, being contradicted, exposed as liars, even ridiculed, but they can never forgive being ignored.
Auberon Waugh, in the *Observer*

Whoever could make two ears of corn or two blades of grass to grow upon a spot of ground where only one grew before would deserve better of mankind and do more essential service to his country than the whole race of politicians put together.
Jonathan Swift

I have found some of the best reasons I ever had for remaining at the bottom simply by looking at the men at the top.
Frank More Colby

He was a man of splendid abilities but utterly corrupt. Like rotten mackerel by moonlight, he shines and stinks.
John Randolph on Edward Livingstone

... and as to you, sir, treacherous in private friendship ... and a hypocrite in public life, the world will be puzzled to decide whether you are an apostate or an impostor, whether you have abandoned good principles, or whether you ever had any?

Tom Paine to George Washington

That dark designing sordid ambitious vain proud arrogant and vindictive knave.

General Charles Lee on George Washington

His attachment to those of his friends whom he could make useful to himself was thoroughgoing and exemplary.

John Quincy Adams on Thomas Jefferson

DEPEW: I hope if it's a girl Mr Taft will name it for his charming wife.

TAFT: If it is a girl, I shall, of course, name it for my lovely helpmate of many years. And if it is a boy, I shall claim the father's prerogative and name it Junior. But if, as I suspect, it is only a bag of wind, I shall name it Chauncey Depew.

William Howard Taft, before his election as President, and Chauncey Depew

He looked at me as if I was a side dish he hadn't ordered.

Ring Lardner, Jr., on President William Howard Taft

Sir, divine providence takes care of his own universe. Moral monsters cannot propagate. Impotent of everything but mal-evolence of purpose, they cannot otherwise multiply miseries than by blaspheming all that is pure and prosperous and happy. Could demon propagate demon, the universe might become a pandemonium; but I rejoice that the Father of Lies can never become the Father of Liars. One adversary of God and man is enough for one universe.

Tristram Burges on US congressman John Randolph, who was widely reputed to be impotent

You pride yourself upon an animal faculty, in respect of which the slave is your equal and the jackass infinitely your superior.
John Randolph to Tristram Burges, in reply to the above

President Robbins was so well adjusted to his environment that sometimes you could not tell which was the environment and which was President Robbins.
Randall Jarrell

Why, if a man were to call my dog McKinley, and the brute failed to resent to the death the damning insult, I'd drown it.
William Cowper Brann on William McKinley

Reader, suppose you were an idiot; and suppose you were a member of Congress; but I repeat myself.
Mark Twain

'Do you pray for the senators, Dr Hale?' 'No, I look at the senators and I pray for the country.'
Edward Everett Hale

The trouble with Senator Long is that he is suffering from halitosis of the intellect.
Harold L. Ickes on Huey Long

[He] stirred whiskey with a thick forefinger, his socks drooped, his suits were green-hued, his ties were indifferent, and his breath was chronically bad. Hunched forward as he talked, he droned on in a flat voice, pronouncing Anthony Eden 'Ant-ny'.
Walter Isaacson and Evan Thomas on John Foster Dulles

The policeman and the trashman call me Alice. You cannot.
Alice Roosevelt Longworth, when Senator Joseph McCarthy called her Alice

The meanest kind of bawling and blowing office-holders, office-seekers, pimps, malignants, conspirators, murderers, fancy-men, custom-house clerks, contractors, kept-editors, spaniels well-train'd to carry and fetch, jobbers, infidels, disunionists, terrorists, mail-riflers, slave-catchers, pushers of slavery, creatures of the President, creatures of would-be Presidents, spies, bribers, compromisers, lobbyers, sponges, ruin'd sports, expell'd gamblers, policy-backers, monte-dealers, duellists, carriers of conceal'd weapons, deaf men, pimpled men, scarr'd inside with vile disease, gaudy outside with gold chains made from the people's money and harlots' money twisted together; crawling, serpentine men, the lousy combinings and born freedom-sellers of the earth.

Walt Whitman on a Democratic National Convention of the 1850s

A man of taste, arrived from Mars, would take one look at the convention floor and leave forever, convinced he had seen one of the drearier squats of Hell ... a cigar-smoking, stale-aired, slack-jawed, butt-littered, foul, bleak, hardworking, bureaucratic death gas of language and faces ... lawyers, judges, ward heelers, mafiosos, Southern goons and grandees, grand old ladies, trade unionists and finks; of pompous words and long pauses which lie like a leaden pain over fever.

Norman Mailer on the Democratic National Convention of 1960

My dear McClellan:

If you don't want to use the army I should like to borrow it for a while. Yours respectfully,

A. Lincoln

Abraham Lincoln to General McClellan, accused of inactivity in the American Civil War

Filthy Story-Teller, Despot, Liar, Thief, Braggart, Buffoon, Usurper, Monster, Ignoramus Abe, Old Scoundrel, Perjurer, Robber, Swindler, Tyrant, Field-Butcher, Land-Pirate.
Harper's Weekly on Abraham Lincoln

His argument is as thin as the homeopathic soup that was made by boiling the shadow of a pigeon that had been starved to death.
Abraham Lincoln on Stephen A. Douglas

His speeches leave the impression of an army of pompous phrases moving over the landscape in search of an idea. Sometimes these meandering words would actually capture a straggling thought and bear it triumphantly, a prisoner in their midst, until it died of servitude and overwork.
Senator William McAdoo on Warren Harding

Deformed Sir, The Ugly Club in full meeting have elected you an honorary member of the Hood-Favored Fraternity. Prince Harry was lean, Falstaff was fat. Thersites was hunchbacked, and Slowkenlengus was renowned for the eminent miscalculation which Nature had made in the length of the nose; but it remained for you to unite all species of deformity and stand forth as The Prince of Ugly Fellows.
Anonymous letter to Abraham Lincoln

McKinley has a chocolate eclair backbone.
Theodore Roosevelt on William McKinley

A Byzantine logothete.
Theodore Roosevelt on Woodrow Wilson

His idea of getting hold of the right end of the stick is to snatch it from the hands of somebody who is using it effectively, and to hit him over the head with it.
George Bernard Shaw on Theodore Roosevelt

Thomas E. Dewey is just about the nastiest little man I've ever known. He struts sitting down.
Mrs Clarence Dykstra

How can they tell?
Dorothy Parker, on being told that Calvin Coolidge was dead

He looks as if he had been weaned on a pickle.
Alice Roosevelt Longworth on Calvin Coolidge

Democracy is that system of government under which the people, having 35,717,342 native-born adult whites to choose from, including thousands who are handsome and many of whom are wise, pick out a Coolidge to be head of state.
H. L. Mencken on Calvin Coolidge

Hoover, if elected, will do one thing that is almost incomprehensible to the human mind: he will make a great man out of Coolidge.
Clarence Darrow during the 1932 American presidential campaign

My choice early in life was either to be a piano-player in a whorehouse or a politician. And to tell the truth, there's hardly any difference.
Harry S Truman

As an intellectual he bestowed upon the games of golf and bridge all the enthusiasm and perseverance that he withheld from books and ideas.
Emmet John Hughes on Dwight David Eisenhower

I guess it proves that in America anyone can be President.
Gerald Ford on his appointment

Roosevelt proved a man could be president for life; Truman proved anybody could be president; and Eisenhower proved we don't need a president.
Anonymous

Mothers all want their sons to grow up to be President but they don't want them to become politicians in the process.
John F. Kennedy

The enviably attractive nephew who sings an Irish ballad for the company and then winsomely disappears before the table-clearing and dishwashing begin.
Lyndon B. Johnson on John F. Kennedy

Lyndon acts like there was never going to be a tomorrow.
Lady Bird Johnson on her husband

I'd much rather have that fellow inside my tent pissing out than outside my tent pissing in.
Lyndon B. Johnson, explaining why he retained J. Edgar Hoover at the FBI

Do you realize the responsibility I carry? I'm the only person standing between Nixon and the White House.
John F. Kennedy to Arthur Schlesinger during the 1960 presidential campaign

Nixon is the kind of politician who would cut down a

redwood tree and then mount the stump to make a speech
for conservation.
Adlai Stevenson on Richard Nixon. Attrib.

Richard Nixon is a no-good lying bastard. He can lie out of
both sides of his mouth at the same time and if he ever caught
himself telling the truth he'd lie just to keep his hand in.
Harry S Truman

Would you buy a second-hand car from this man?
Mort Sahl on Richard Nixon. Attrib.

Nixon, pull out like your father should have.
Graffiti on Richard Nixon

Richard Nixon is a pubic hair in the teeth of America.
Graffiti on Richard Nixon

Jerry Ford is so dumb that he can't fart and chew gum at the
same time.
Lyndon B. Johnson on Gerald Ford

Jerry Ford is a nice guy, but he played too much football with
his helmet off.
Lyndon B. Johnson on Gerald Ford

He looks like the guy in a science fiction movie who is the
first to see the Creature.
David Frye on Gerald Ford

I love all my children, but some of them I don't like.
Lillian Carter, mother of Jimmy Carter

A hippie is someone who looks like Tarzan, walks like Jane and smells like Cheetah.
Ronald Reagan

A triumph of the embalmer's art.
Gore Vidal on Ronald Reagan

Not only a barbarian, but flaky.
Ronald Reagan on Colonel Muammar Gaddafi

They never open their mouths without subtracting from the sum of human knowledge.
Thomas Reed, Speaker of the House of Representatives, on members of Congress

The world would not be in such a snarl,
Had Marx been Groucho instead of Karl.
Irving Berlin on Karl Marx

As with the Christian religion, the worst advertisement for Socialism is its adherents.
George Orwell

Russian communism is the illegitimate child of Karl Marx and Catherine the Great.
Clement Attlee

I offer a toast to this gracious lady. Up your bottom.
Andrei Gromyko, Soviet Foreign Minister, to Mrs Dean Rusk at the 1979 Vienna Summit, after he had refused the assistance of a translator

A pig-eyed bag of wind.
Frank L. Howley on Nikita Khrushchev

When you are skinning your customers, you should leave some on to grow so that you can skin them again.
Nikita Khrushchev to British businessmen

The Pope! How many divisions has *he* got?
Joseph Stalin, when urged by Pierre Laval to tolerate Catholicism in the USSR to appease the Pope

Pathological exhibits ... human scum ... paranoics, degenerates, morons, bludgers ... pack of dingoes ... industrial outlaws and political lepers ... ratbags. If these people went to Russia, Stalin wouldn't even use them for manure.
Arthur Calwell, Australian Minister of Immigration and Information, on Australian Communists

That all men are equal is a proposition to which, at ordinary times, no sane individual has ever given his assent.
Aldous Huxley, *Proper Studies*

Stupid asses.
Karl Marx and Friedrich Engels on the proletariat, private correspondence

We will bury you.
Nikita Khrushchev at a Kremlin reception

This war, like the next war, is a war to end war.
David Lloyd George on the First World War

You can't say civilization don't advance, however, for in every war they kill you a new way.
Will Rogers, *Autobiography*

War is the national industry of Prussia.
Honoré Gabriel Riquetti, Comte de Mirabeau. Attrib.

If I were fierce, and bald, and short of breath,
   I'd live with scarlet Majors at the Base,
And speed glum heroes up to the line to death.
   You'd see me with my puffy petulant face,
Guzzling and gulping in the best hotel,
   Reading the Roll of Honour. 'Poor young chap,'
I'd say – 'I used to know his father well;
   Yes, we've lost heavily in this last scrap.'
And when the war is done and youth stone dead,
I'd toddle safely home and die – in bed.

Siegfried Sassoon, *Counter-Attack*, 'Base Details'

There they are cutting each other's throats, because one half of them prefer hiring their servants for life, and the other by the hour.

Thomas Carlyle on the American Civil War. Attrib.

Patriots always talk of dying for their country, and never of killing for their country.

Bertrand Russell

A soldier is a man whose business it is to kill those who never offended him, and who are the innocent martyrs of other men's iniquities. Whatever may become of the abstract question of the justifiableness of war, it seems impossible that the soldier should not be a depraved and unnatural thing.

William Godwin

War hath no fury like a non-combatant.

C. E. Montague, *Disenchantment*

The DAILY HERALD
Is unkind.
It has been horrid
About my nice new war.
I shall burn the DAILY HERALD.

I think, myself,
That my new war
Is one of the nicest we've had;
It is not war really,
It is only a training for the next one,
And saves the expense
Of Army Manoeuvres.
Besides, we have not declared war;
We are merely restoring order –
As the Germans did in Belgium,
And as I hope to do later
In Ireland.
I never really liked
The late Tsar;
He was very weak and reactionary...

As I said in a great speech
After the last great war,
I begin to fear
That the nation's heroic mood
Is over.
Only three years ago
I was allowed to waste
A million lives in Gallipoli,
But now

War & the generals

They object
To my gambling
With a few thousand men
In Russia!
It does seem a shame.
I shall burn the DAILY HERALD.
Osbert Sitwell, 'A Certain Statesman' (Churchill), in the *Daily Herald*, 1919

Lions led by donkeys.
Max Hoffmann on the British army in the First World War

Ours is composed of the scum of the earth.
Duke of Wellington on the British army

I don't know what effect these men will have on the enemy,
but, by God, they terrify me.
Duke of Wellington on his troops

Jellicoe was the only man on either side who could lose the
war in an afternoon.
Winston Churchill

He never commanded more than ten men in his life – and he
ate three of them.
General Weston on Adolphus Greely, upon his being made a general. Much
of his life had been spent as an Arctic explorer

If Kitchener was not a great man, he was, at least, a great
poster.
Margot Asquith

The General is suffering from mental saddle sores.
Harold L. Ickes on Huey Long

He really deserves some sort of decoration … a medal inscribed 'For Vaguery in the Field'.
John Osborne, *Look Back in Anger*

In defeat unbeatable; in victory unbearable.
Winston Churchill on Viscount Montgomery

Don't talk to me about naval tradition. It's nothing but rum, sodomy, and the lash.
Winston Churchill

The British soldier can stand up to anything except the British War Office.
George Bernard Shaw

One to mislead the public, another to mislead the Cabinet, and the third to mislead itself.
Herbert Asquith, explaining why the War Office kept three sets of figures

Maybe it would have been better if neither of us had been born.
Napoleon Bonaparte, looking at the tomb of Jean-Jacques Rousseau

The Falklands thing was a fight between two bald men over a comb.
Jorge Luis Borges on the Falklands War

Imperialist running dogs.
Approved Chinese term for Americans in print and on radio

A crew of pirates are driven by a storm they know not whither; at length a boy discovers land from the topmast; they go on shore to rob and plunder; they see a harmless people, are entertained with kindness; they give the country a new name;

they take formal possession of it for their king; they set up a rotten plank or a stone for a memorial; they murder two or three dozen natives; bring away a couple more by force for a sample; return home and get their pardon. Here commences a new dominion acquired with a title by divine right. Ships are sent with the first opportunity; the natives driven out or destroyed; their princes tortured to discover their gold; a free licence given to all acts of inhumanity and lust, the earth reeking with the blood of its inhabitants: and this execrable crew of butchers, employed in so pious an expedition, is a modern colony, sent to convert and civilize an idolatrous and barbarous people.

Jonathan Swift, *Gulliver's Travels*. Gulliver on the English system of colonizing

Civilized men arrived in the Pacific, armed with alcohol, syphilis, trousers, and the Bible.

Havelock Ellis

They send all their troops to drain the products of industry, to seize all the treasures, wealth and prosperity of the country. Like a vulture with their harpy talons grappled in the vitals of the land, they flap away the lesser kites and they call it protection. It is the protection of the vultures to the lamb.

Richard Brinsley Sheridan on the East India Company

Columbus was not a learned man, but an ignorant. He was not an honourable man, but a professional pirate . . . His voyage was undertaken with a view solely to his own advantage, the gratification of an incredible avarice. In the lust of gold he committed deeds of cruelty, treachery and oppression for which no fitting names are found in the vocabulary of any

modern tongue. To the harmless and hospitable peoples among whom he came he was a terror and a curse...
Ambrose Bierce on Christopher Columbus

I admire him, I frankly confess it; and when his time comes I shall buy a piece of the rope for a keepsake.
Mark Twain on Cecil Rhodes

It is nauseating to see Mr Gandhi, a seditious Middle Temple lawyer, now posing as a fakir of a type well known in the East, striding half naked up the steps of the Viceregal Palace, while he is still organizing and conducting a defiant campaign of civil disobedience, to parley with the representative of the King Emperor.
Winston Churchill on Mahatma Gandhi

I think it would be a good idea.
Mahatma Gandhi on being asked his view of Western civilization. Attrib.

Gandhi was very keen on sex. He renounced it when he was 36, so thereafter it was never very far from his thoughts.
Woodrow Wyatt on Mahatma Gandhi

I am sure that Dickie has done marvellously. But it is curious that we should regard as a hero the man who liquidated the Empire which other heroes such as Clive, Warren Hastings, and Napier won for us. Very odd indeed.
Harold Nicolson on Earl Mountbatten

[He] speaks like a Buddha and thinks like a serpent ... His soul is possessed by British colonialism. Nothing can distract him from his perfidy ... The truth has come to light ... Chris Patten will stand condemned down the ages.
Wen Wei Po, the Communist-run newspaper in Hong Kong, on Chris Patten, the Governor

This democracy knows you as the poisoner of the streams of human intercourse, the fomenter of war, the preacher of hate, the unscrupulous enemy of human society.
A. G. Gardner on the publisher Lord Northcliffe

They are only ten.
Lord Northcliffe, notice to remind the staff on his newspapers of the mental age of the general public.

A single sentence will suffice for modern man: he fornicated and read the papers.
Albert Camus, *The Fall*

We live under a government of men and morning newspapers.
Wendell Phillips

A journalist is a person who works harder than any other lazy person in the world.
Anonymous

A foreign correspondent is someone who flies around from hotel to hotel and thinks that the most interesting thing about any story is the fact that he has arrived to cover it.
Tom Stoppard, *Night and Day*

Every journalist who is not too stupid or too full of himself to notice what is going on knows that what he does is morally indefensible. He is a kind of confidence man, preying on people's vanity, ignorance, or loneliness, gaining their trust and betraying them without remorse.
Janet Malcolm

You cannot hope
to bribe or twist,
thank God! the
British journalist.

But, seeing what
the man will do
unbribed, there's
no occasion to.
Humbert Wolfe

Once a newspaper touches a story, the facts are lost for ever,
even to the protagonists.
Norman Mailer

I read the newspaper avidly. It is my one form of continuous
fiction.
Aneurin Bevan

You lying BBC; you're photographing things that aren't
happening.
Belfast woman to a BBC cameraman

Sir: During the short time since the *Sun* started publishing in
Edmonton, I have witnessed your decay from amiable drunk
through voyeur and track rat to misogynous, vitriolic pariah
... I cannot but from now on dismiss your scribblings as the
libelous drivel of an unbalanced mind.
Robert Hamilton, letter to the *Edmonton Sun*

I can but wonder what will become of the editor of the Los
Angeles *Times* when the breath leaves his feculent body and
death stops the rattling of his abortive brain. He cannot be

buried at sea lest he poison the fishes. He cannot be suspended in mid-air, like Mahomet's coffin, lest the circling wolds, in their endeavor to avoid contamination, crash together, wreck the universe and bring about the reign of chaos and Old Night. The damn scoundrel is a white elephant on the hands of the Deity, and I have some curiosity to know what He will do with him.

William Cowper Brann

All newspaper editorial writers ever do is come down from the hills after the battle is over and bayonet the wounded.

Anonymous

An editor is one who separates the wheat from the chaff and prints the chaff.

Adlai Stevenson

The Times is speechless and takes three columns to express its speechlessness.

Winston Churchill on Irish Home Rule

On the whole I would not say that our Press is obscene. I would say that it trembles on the brink of obscenity.

Lord Longford

Journalism consists in buying white paper at two cents a pound and selling it for ten cents a pound.

Cyril Connolly

There is much to be said in favour of modern journalism. By giving us the opinions of the uneducated, it keeps us in touch with the ignorance of the community.

Oscar Wilde

No one ever went broke underestimating the taste of the American public.
H. L. Mencken

There is not a more mean, stupid, dastardly, pitiful, selfish, envious, ungrateful animal than the public. It is the greatest of cowards, for it is afraid of itself.
William Hazlitt, 'On Living to Oneself'

Teenage scribblers.
Nigel Lawson, when Chancellor, on City journalists

It's great to be with Bill Buckley, because you don't have to think. He takes a position and you automatically take the opposite one and you know you're right.
John Kenneth Galbraith on William F. Buckley, Jr., right-wing editor of the *National Review*

Price of Herald three cents daily. Five cents Sunday. Bennett.
Telegram from James Gordon Bennett, American newspaper owner and editor, to William Randolph Hearst, when Hearst, who was trying to buy his paper, asked for a price

If Max gets to Heaven he won't last long. He will be chucked out for trying to pull off a merger between Heaven and Hell . . . after having secured a controlling interest in key subsidiary companies in both places, of course.
H. G. Wells on Lord Beaverbrook

A legend in his own lunchtime.
Christopher Wordsworth on the journalist Clifford Makins

His improbabilities started with his looks. His long body seemed to be only basted together, his hair was quills upon the fretful porcupine, his teeth were Stonehenge, his clothes looked as if they had been brought up by somebody else.

Dorothy Parker on Harold Ross, editor of the *New Yorker*

I think we fell out when you said 'I think' and I said 'I don't give a fuck what you think'.

Kelvin Mackenzie, former editor of the *Sun*, to a marketing man at the latter's leaving party

Well tell him to go take a flying fuck at a rolling doughnut.

Kelvin Mackenzie to a colleague worried lest Mackenzie upset another editor

Switch off now. There's no sex in this programme, unless you count the *Sun* newspaper's dirty words, but there will be a great deal of violence. I'm going to get down there in the gutter where so many of our journalists crawl, and for maybe the third time in my life conduct an argument in the sort of personal terms that have become the norm across such large and fetid tracks of our cynical, venal, genuinely prostituted and foreign-owned Press.

Touch and go though it has been, and through an often messy and occasionally shameful personal life, I've managed to gather around myself some shreds of self-respect, so what I'm about to do is perhaps less obviously foolhardy than it otherwise might seem. And what I am about to do is to make a provenly vindictive and extremely powerful enemy, a sort of serial killer (metaphorically speaking) who has more phials of poison at his command than there are chemists' shops in this troubled land.

This programme is not going out live, so at least I know that I shall reach the end of it in more or less one piece. Not *quite* a joke – more a nervous simper – because the enemy in question is that drivel-merchant, global huckster and so-to-speak media psychopath Rupert Murdoch, a Hannibal The Cannibal who is in many important ways a deal more powerful in Britain than our own schoolboy Parliament, its minority-elected Government, and even its bumbling Mr Pooter of a Prime Minister. A Government – and God help us – that the Murdoch Press did so much, so dishonestly, to put into power, mostly by means so aslant, so titled, so bent and untrue that they by definition open the trap-door under the word 'democracy'. If we cared twopence about our own culture, we ought to make sure that the next time Murdoch sets foot in this, his fiefdom, he should be arrested and put on public trial . . .

In less than an hour's time on this channel, there will be another episode of *Lipstick On Your Collar*. Let darkness fall upon the land, and England's mountains green be splattered with used condoms, for the series is written by that lecherous beast known to the toilet-paper papers as Dirty Den, or by Murdoch's salacious *News of the World* as 'Television's Mr Filth', or, in an endearing reference to what must be my other less priapic illness by that sub-literate, homophobic, sniggering rictus of a lout Gary Bushell of Murdoch's 'The *Sun*', *Old Flakey*. 'Very Lipstick on my dipstick', slurps Bushell, with the kind of saloon-bar leer that presumably adds some kind of balance to what one might charitably call his Talent, all of which you could just about press into the little space you get when you lift a plastic lavatory brush from its holder.

Dennis Potter on tabloid journalism, on Channel 4, 1993

A mere ulcer; a sore from head to foot; a poor devil so completely flayed that there is not a square inch of healthy flesh on his carcass; an overgrown pimple, sore to the touch.

Quarterly Review on William Hazlitt

Sir, – You have an ugly trick of saying what is not true of any one you do not like; and it will be the object of this letter to cure you of it. You say what you please of others: it is time you were told what you are. In doing this, give me leave to borrow the familiarity of your style – for the fidelity of the picture I shall be answerable.

You are a little person, but a considerable cat's-paw; and so far worthy of notice. Your clandestine connexion with persons high in office constantly influences your opinions, and alone gives importance to them. You are the *Government Critic*, a character nicely differing from that of a government spy – the invisible link, that connects literature with the police. It is your business to keep a strict eye over all writers who differ in opinion with His Majesty's Ministers, and to measure their talents and attainments by the standard of their servility and meanness. For this office you are well qualified. Besides being the Editor of the *Quarterly Review*, you are also paymaster of the band of Gentlemen Pensioners; and when an author comes before you in the one capacity, with whom you are not acquainted in the other, you know how to deal with him. You have your cue beforehand. The distinction between truth and falsehood you make no account of: you mind only the distinction between Whig and Tory. Accustomed to the indulgence of your mercenary virulence and party-spite, you have lost all relish as well as capacity for the unperverted exercises of the understanding, and make up for the obvious want of ability by a bare-faced want of principle. The same set of threadbare common-places, the same second-hand assortment of abusive nick-names, the same assumption of little magisterial airs of superiority, are regularly repeated; and the ready convenient lie comes in aid of the dearth of other resources, and passes off, with impunity, in the garb of religion and loyalty...

... There is something in your nature and habits that fits you for the situation into which your good fortune has thrown you. In the first place, you are in no danger of exciting the jealousy of your patrons by a mortifying display of extraordinary talents, while your sordid devotion to their will and to your own interest at once ensures their gratitude and contempt. To crawl and lick the dust is all they expect of you, and all you can do. Otherwise they might fear your power, for they could have no dependence on your fidelity: but they take you with safety and fondness to their bosoms; for they know if you cease to be a tool, you cease to be anything. If you had an exuberance of wit, the unguarded use of it might sometimes glance at your employers; if you were sincere yourself, you might respect the motives of others; if you had sufficient understanding, you might attempt an argument, and fail in it. But luckily for yourself and your admirers, you are but the dull echo, 'the tenth transmitter' of some hackneyed jest: the want of all manly and candid feeling in yourself only excites your suspicion and antipathy to it in others, as something at which your nature recoils: your slowness to understand makes you quick to misrepresent; and you infallibly make nonsense of what you cannot possibly conceive.

What seem your wilful blunders are often the felicity of natural parts, and your want of penetration has all the appearance of an affected petulance! . . .

Such, Sir, is the picture of which you have sat for the outline.

William Hazlitt, 'A Letter to William Gifford', editor of the *Quarterly Review*

Has there ever been a more confusing face? With an expression half-bovine and half sheep-like he stares out of the screen in such a way as to leave us all uncertain whether he wants to cut our throats or lick our boots.

Peregrine Worsthorne on *Sunday Times* editor Andrew Neil, in the *Sunday Telegraph*

That is a bit rich coming from a man who looks like a sexually confused, ageing hairdresser: the Teasy Weasy of Fleet Street . . .

Richard Littlejohn, in the *Sun*, on Peregrine Worsthorne after the latter's attack on Andrew Neil

The reciprocal civility of authors is one of the most risible scenes in the farce of life.

Samuel Johnson, 'Life of Sir Thomas Browne'

Chuang Tzu was born in the fourth century before Christ. The publication of this book in English, two thousand years after his death, is obviously premature.

Anonymous

All the universities and all the old writers put together are less talented than my arsehole.

Theophrastus Bombastus von Hohenheim, known as Paracelsus, German alchemist and physician, to his critics

I am sure I have only slightly less high an opinion of Matthew's
literary ability than he does himself.
Alan Lomberg, the editor's English teacher in Swaziland, in a school report

Critics! appall'd I venture on the name,
Those cut-throat bandits in the path of fame.
Robert Burns

If you imagine a Scotch commercial traveller in a Scotch
commercial hotel leaning on the bar and calling the barmaid
'Dearie' then you will know the keynote of Burns' verse.
A. E. Housman on Robert Burns

Thou eunuch of language ... thou pimp of gender ... murderous accoucheur of infant learning ... thou pickle-herring
in the puppet show of nonsense.
Robert Burns on a critic

I think of Mr Stevenson as a consumptive youth weaving
garlands of sad flowers with pale, weak hands.
George Moore on Robert Louis Stevenson

That vague formless obscene face.
Oscar Wilde on George Moore

Henry James writes fiction as if it were a painful duty.
Oscar Wilde

He has a gross and repulsive face but appears *bon enfant* when
you talk to him. But he is the dullest Briton of them all.
Henry James on Anthony Trollope

The work of Henry James has always seemed divisible by a

simple dynastic arrangement into three reigns. James I, James
II, and the Old Pretender.
Philip Guedalla

It's not that he 'bites off more than he can chew' but he chews
more than he bites off.
Clover Adams on Henry James

He was unperfect, unfinished, inartistic; he was worse than
provincial – he was parochial.
Henry James on Henry David Thoreau

I doubt that the infant monster has any more to give.
Henry James on Rudyard Kipling

Poor Henry James! He's spending eternity walking round and
round a stately park and the fence is just too high for him to
peep over and he's just too far away to hear what the countess
is saying.
W. Somerset Maugham

Henry James has a mind so fine that no idea could violate it.
T. S. Eliot. Attrib.

Mr Eliot is at times an excellent poet and has arrived at the
supreme Eminence among English critics largely through
disguising himself as a corpse.
Ezra Pound on T. S. Eliot

To me Pound remains the exquisite showman minus the *show*.
Ben Hecht on Ezra Pound

A hack writer who would not have been considered fourth
rate in Europe, who tried out a few of the old proven 'sure-

fire' literary skeletons with sufficient local colour to intrigue
the superficial and the lazy.
William Faulkner on Mark Twain

Jane Austen's books, too, are absent from this library. Just that
one omission alone would make a fairly good library out of a
library that hadn't a book in it.
Mark Twain

I have discovered that our great favourite, Miss Austen, is my
countryman . . . with whom Mama, before her marriage, was
acquainted. Mama says that she was then the prettiest, silliest,
most affected, husband-hunting butterfly she ever remembers.
Mary Russell Mitford on Jane Austen, letter to a friend

I found out in the first two pages that it was a woman's
writing – she supposed that in making a door, you last of all
put in the panels!
Thomas Carlyle on *Adam Bede* by George Eliot

I wish her characters would talk a little less like the heroes and
heroines of police reports.
George Eliot on *Jane Eyre* by Charlotte Brontë

All the faults of *Jane Eyre* are magnified a thousandfold, and
the only consolation which we have in reflecting upon it is
that it will never be generally read.
James Lorimer on *Wuthering Heights* by Emily Brontë, in the *North British Review*

Literature cannot be the business of a woman's life, because
of the sacredness of her duties at home.
Robert Southey on Charlotte Brontë

Oh really. What is she reading?
Dame Edith Evans to a friend who said Nancy Mitford was borrowing her
villa in France to finish a book

A woman who writes a book commits two sins; she increases
the number of books, and decreases the number of women.
Alphonse Karr

One of the surest signs of his genius is that women dislike his
books.
George Orwell on Joseph Conrad

He would not blow his nose without moralizing on conditions
in the handkerchief industry.
Cyril Connolly on George Orwell

One could always baffle Conrad by saying 'humour'. It was
one of our damned English tricks he had never learned to
tackle.
H. G. Wells on Joseph Conrad

He is the old maid among novelists.
Rebecca West on H. G. Wells

His writing, as he might have said himself, is like lace; the
material is of very little consequence, the embroidery is all
that counts; and it shares with lace the happy faculty of coming
out sometimes in yards and yards.
Lytton Strachey on Horace Walpole

He has the most remarkable and seductive genius – and I
should say about the smallest in the world.
Lytton Strachey on Max Beerbohm

Of course we all know that Morris was a wonderful all-round man, but the act of walking round him has always tired me.
Max Beerbohm on William Morris

The gods bestowed on Max the gift of perpetual old age.
Oscar Wilde on Max Beerbohm

Tell me, when you are alone with Max, does he take off his face and reveal his mask?
Oscar Wilde on Max Beerbohm

One must have a heart of stone to read the death of little Nell without laughing.
Oscar Wilde on Charles Dickens's *Old Curiosity Shop*

He's a mediocre man – and knows it, or suspects it, which is worse; he will come to no good, and in the meantime he's treated rudely by waiters and is not really admired even by middle-aged dowagers.
Lytton Strachey on E. M. Forster

My knowledge of Mr Forster's work is limited to one novel which I dislike, and anyway it was not he who fathered that trite little whimsy about characters getting out of hand, it is as old as the quills, although, of course, one sympathizes with his people if they try to wriggle out of that trip to India or wherever he takes them. My characters are all galley-slaves.
Vladimir Nabokov on E. M. Forster, *The Paris Review Interviews*

A novelist who writes nothing for 10 years finds his reputation rising. Because I keep on producing books they say there must be something wrong with this fellow.
J. B. Priestley

He is limp and damp and milder than the breath of a cow.
Virginia Woolf on E. M. Forster

I thought nothing of her writing. I considered her a beautiful
little knitter.
Edith Sitwell on Virginia Woolf

She had been a peculiar kind of snob without really belonging
to a social group with whom to be snobbish.
Edmund Wilson on Virginia Woolf

The first 200 pages of Ulysses . . . Never have I read such tosh.
As for the first two chapters we will let them pass, but the
3rd, 4th, 5th, 6th – merely the scratchings of pimples on the
body of the bootboy at Claridges.
Virginia Woolf on *Ulysses* by James Joyce

The work of a queasy undergraduate scratching his pimples.
Virginia Woolf on *Ulysses* by James Joyce

The last part of it is the dirtiest, most indecent, most obscene
thing ever written. Yes it is, Frieda . . . it is filthy. My god,
what a clumsy 'olla putrida' James Joyce is! Nothing but old
fags and cabbage-stumps of quotations from the Bible and
the rest, stewed in the juice of deliberate, journalistic dirty-
mindedness.
D. H. Lawrence on *Ulysses* by James Joyce

We have met too late. You are too old for me to have any
effect on you.
James Joyce on meeting W. B. Yeats

Dear Mr Pinker,
    I have read the effusion of Mr Duckworth's reader with

not inconsiderable disgust. These vermin crawl over and be-s-lime our literature with their pulings, and nothing but the day of judgement can, I suppose, exterminate 'em. Thank god one need not, under ordinary circumstances, touch them. Hark to his puling squeak: too 'unconventional'. What in hell do we want but some change from the unbearable monotony of the weekly six shilling pears soap annual novel; . . . the dungminded dungbearded, penny a line, please the mediocre-at-all-cost doctrine. You English will get no prose till you enterminate [sic] this breed . . .

Canting, supercilious, blockhead . . . I always supposed from report that Duckworth was an educated man, but I can not reconcile this opinion with his retention of the author of the missive you send me. If you have to spend your life in contact with such minds, God help you . . .

Why can't you send the publisher's reader to the serbian front, and get some good out of the war . . .

Serious writers will certainly give up the use of english altogether unless you can improve the process of publication.

In conclusion, you have given me a very unpleasant quarter of an hour, my disgust flows over, though I suppose there is no use in spreading it over this paper. If there is any phrase or form of contempt that you care to convey from me to the reeking Malebolge of the Duckworthian slum, pray, consider yourself at liberty to draw on my account (unlimited credit) and transmit it.

Please, if you have occasion to write again, either in regard to this book or any other, please do not enclose the publisher's readers opinions. Sincerely yours,
EZRA POUND

P.S. . . . as for altering Joyce to suit Duckworth's readers – I would like trying to fit the Venus de Milo into a piss-pot . . .

Ezra Pound, acting for James Joyce, to the literary agent James B. Pinker. The reader for the publisher, Duckworth, had complained that Joyce's *Portrait of the Artist as a Young Man* was 'too discursive, formless, unrestrained', and that 'ugly things, ugly words, are too prominent; indeed at times they seem to be shoved in one's face on purpose unnecessarily'.

Why don't you write books people can read?

Mrs Nora Joyce to her husband, James

An essentially private man who wished his total indifference to public notice to be universally recognized.

Tom Stoppard on James Joyce

He had a genius for backing into the limelight.

Lowell Thomas, biographer of T. E. Lawrence

I fancy, for myself, that they are rather out of touch with reality; by reality I mean shops like Selfridges, and motor buses, and the *Daily Express*.

T. E. Lawrence on expatriate authors living in Paris, such as James Joyce, in a letter to W. Hurley

Arabian Lawrence, who, whatever his claims as a man, was surely a sonorous fake as a writer.

Kingsley Amis on T. E. Lawrence

A bore and a bounder and a prig. He was intoxicated with his own youth, and loathed any milieu which he couldn't dominate. Certainly he had none of a gentleman's instincts, strutting about Peace Conferences in Arab dress.

Sir Henry Channon on T. E. Lawrence

It seems that Dr Leavis gave a lecture at Nottingham University on 'Literature In My Time' and declared that apart from D. H. Lawrence there has been no literature in his time. He knocked hell out of everybody, and no doubt had all the Lucky Jims rolling down the aisles. Like Groucho Marx on another academic occasion, whatever it was he was against it. Virginia Woolf was a 'slender talent'; Lytton Strachey 'irresponsible and unscrupulous'; W. H. Auden 'the career type', fixed at 'the undergraduate stage'; Spender 'no talent whatsoever'; Day-Lewis 'Book Society author'; the whole age 'dismal', and outlook 'very poor'. By the time Dr Leavis caught his train back to Cambridge, there was hardly anything left to read in Nottingham. I have not the pleasure of the doctor's acquaintance – he was up at Cambridge just after me – but I have a vague but impressive vision of him, pale and glittering-eyed, shining with integrity, marching out of Downing to close whole departments of libraries, to snatch books out of people's hands, to proclaim the bitter truth that nobody writes anything worth reading. There is Lawrence; there is Leavis on Lawrence; perhaps a disciple, Jones, is writing something – let us say, Jones on Leavis on Lawrence; after that, nothing.

J. B. Priestley on F. R. Leavis

It is sad to see Milton's great lines bobbing up and down in the sandy desert of Dr Leavis's mind with the grace of a fleet of weary camels.

Edith Sitwell on F. R. Leavis, *Aspects of Modern Poetry*

Then Edith Sitwell appeared, her nose longer than an ant-eater's, and read some of her absurd stuff.

Lytton Strachey, 'An evening at Arnold Bennett's House'

I do not want Miss Mannin's feelings to be hurt by the fact that I have never heard of her. At the moment I am debarred from the pleasures of putting her in her place by the fact she has not got one.
Edith Sitwell on Ethel Mannin

So you've been reviewing Edith Sitwell's last piece of virgin dung, have you? Isn't she a poisonous thing of a woman, lying, concealing, flipping, plagiarizing, misquoting, and being as clever a crooked literary publicist as ever.
Dylan Thomas on Edith Sitwell

He was a detestable man. Men pressed money on him, and women their bodies. Dylan took both with equal contempt. His great pleasure was to humiliate people.
A. J. P. Taylor on Dylan Thomas

Somebody's boring me. I think it's me.
Dylan Thomas after he had been talking continuously for some time

I loathe you. You revolt me stewing in your consumption.
D. H. Lawrence to Katherine Mansfield

Spit on her when you see her, she's a liar out and out. As for him, I reserve my language ... vermin, the pair of 'em.
D. H. Lawrence on Katherine Mansfield and J. Middleton Murry

Interesting, but a type I could not get on with. Obsessed with self. Dead eyes and a red beard, long narrow face. A strange bird.
John Galsworthy on D. H. Lawrence

Like a piece of litmus paper he has always been quick to take the colour of the times.

The *Observer* on Aldous Huxley

You could tell by his conversation which volume of the Encyclopaedia Britannica he'd been reading. One day it would be Alps, Andes and Apennines, and the next it would be the Himalayas and the Hippocratic Oath.

Bertrand Russell on Aldous Huxley

Mr Douglas would rather give a child prussic acid than allow it to read *The Well of Loneliness* ... I offered to provide Mr Douglas with a child, a bottle of prussic acid, a copy of *The Well of Loneliness*, and – if he kept his word and chose to administer the acid – a handsome memorial in marble to be erected wherever he might appoint, after his execution. The offer, I regret to say, was not accepted.

Aldous Huxley on James Douglas

Your manuscript is both good and original; but the part that is good is not original, and the part that is original is not good.

Samuel Johnson

I hate a fellow whom pride, or cowardice, or laziness drives into a corner, and who does nothing when he is there but sit and *growl*; let him come out as I do, and *bark*.

Samuel Johnson

There is no arguing with Johnson; for when his pistol misses fire, he knocks you down with the butt end of it.

Oliver Goldsmith on Samuel Johnson

Curse the blasted, jelly-boned swines, the slimy, the belly-wriggling invertebrates, the miserable sodding rotters, the flaming sods, the snivelling, dribbling, dithering, palsied, pulseless lot that make up England. They've got white of egg in their veins, and their spunk is that watery it's a marvel they can breed. Why, why, why, was I born an Englishman!

D. H. Lawrence after a publisher rejected his manuscript of *Sons and Lovers*

I like to write when I feel spiteful: it's like having a good sneeze.

D. H. Lawrence, review of *Art-Nonsense* by Eric Gill, in the *Phoenix*

My publisher and I visited your establishment several weeks ago and found you such a preposterous boor that I was moved to discourse upon the likes of you in the attached interview with the *Washington Star*. The next time I am in Paris I intend to spread cream cheese all over your collection.

Letter to George Whitman, proprietor of Shakespeare & Co in Paris, from an American lady

I am only one, only one, only one. Only one being, one at the same time. Not two, not three, only one. Only one life to live, only sixty minutes in one hour. Only one pair of eyes. Only one brain. Only one being. Being only one, having only one pair of eyes, having only one time, having only one life, I cannot read your MS three or four times. Not even one time. Only one look, only one look is enough. Hardly one copy would sell here. Hardly one. Hardly one.

A. J. Fifield, rejecting a manuscript by Gertrude Stein

Gertrude Stein's prose is a cold, black suet-pudding. We can represent it as a cold suet-roll of fabulously reptilian length.

Cut it at any point, it is ... the same heavy, sticky, opaque mass all through, and all along.

Percy Wyndham Lewis

I do not think I have ever seen a nastier-looking man ... Under the black hat, when I had first seen them, the eyes had been those of an unsuccessful rapist.

Ernest Hemingway on Percy Wyndham Lewis

He is the bully on the Left Bank, always ready to twist the milksop's arm.

Cyril Connolly on Ernest Hemingway

Sing a song of critics
pockets full of lye
four and twenty critics
hope that you will die
hope that you will peter out
hope that you will fail
so they can be the first one
be the first to hail
any happy weakening or sign of quick decay ...
If you do not like them lads
one thing you can do
stick them up your asses lads
My Valentine to you.

Ernest Hemingway, 'Valentine – for a Mr Lee Wilson Dodd and Any of His Friends Who Want It'. Wilson Dodd had given Hemingway's *Men without Women* a poor review in the *Saturday Review of Literature*

If my books had been any worse I should not have been

invited to Hollywood, and if they had been any better I should not have come.
Raymond Chandler

Another damned, thick, square book! Always scribble, scribble, scribble! Eh! Mr Gibbon?
William, Duke of Gloucester, to Edward Gibbon

In some passages he drew the thread of his verbosity finer than the staple of his argument.
Richard Porson on Edward Gibbon

Gibbon is an ugly, affected, disgusting fellow, and poisons our literary club for me. I class him among infidel wasps and enormous snakes.
James Boswell on Edward Gibbon

That he was a coxcomb and a bore, weak, vain, pushing, curious, garrulous, was obvious to all who were acquainted with him. That he could not reason, that he had no wit, no humour, no eloquence, is apparent from his writings. Nature had made him a slave and an idolater. His mind resembled those creepers which the botanists call parasites and which can subsist only by clinging round the stems and imbibing the juices of stronger plants.

Servile and impertinent, shallow and pedantic, a bigot and a sot, bloated with family pride, and eternally blustering about the dignity of a born gentleman, yet stooping to be a tablebearer, an eavesdropper, a common butt in the taverns of London ... Everything which another man would have hidden, everything the publication of which would have made another man hang himself, was a matter of exaltation to his weak and diseased mind.

Thomas Babington Macaulay on James Boswell

I wish I was as cocksure of anything as Tom Macaulay is of everything.

Lord Melbourne on Thomas Babington Macaulay

You know, when I am gone you will be sorry you never heard me speak.

Sydney Smith to Thomas Babington Macaulay, a non-stop talker

CONCERNED LADY: Oo poor 'ickle fing, did oo hurt oo's 'ickle finger then?
MACAULAY, AGED 4:   Thank you, Madam, but the agony has somewhat abated.

Thomas Babington Macaulay, quoted in Wanda Orton's biography

The great apostle of the Philistines.

Matthew Arnold, referring to Thomas Babington Macaulay

He not only overflowed with learning, but stood in the slop.

Sydney Smith on Thomas Babington Macaulay

Rogers is not very well ... Don't you know he has produced a couplet? When he is delivered of a couplet, with infinite labour and pain, he takes to his bed, has straw laid down, the knocker tied up, expects his friends to call and make enquiries, and the answer at the door invariably is 'Mr Rogers and his little couplet are as well as can be expected.' When he produces an Alexandrine he keeps to his bed a day longer.

Sydney Smith on Samuel Rogers

Literature

It is long yet vigorous, like the penis of a jackass.
Sydney Smith on an article in the *Edinburgh Review* by Henry Brougham

Chesterton is like a vile scum on a pond ... All his slop – it is really modern catholicism to a great extent, the *never* taking a hedge straight, the mumbo-jumbo of superstition dodging behind clumsy fun and paradox ... I believe he creates a milieu in which art is impossible. He and his kind.
Ezra Pound on G. K. Chesterton

Reading Proust is like bathing in someone else's dirty water.
Alexander Woollcott on Marcel Proust. Attrib.

Monsieur Zola is determined to show that if he has not genius he can at least be dull.
Oscar Wilde

A fat little flabby person with the face of a baker, the clothes of a cobbler, the size of a barrelmaker, the manners of a stocking salesman, and the dress of an innkeeper.
Victor de Balabin on Honoré de Balzac, *Diary*

Authors are easy to get on with – if you're fond of children.
Michael Joseph, publisher

This is not a novel to be tossed aside lightly. It should be thrown with great force.
Dorothy Parker on Benito Mussolini's *Claudia Particella, L'Amante del Cardinale: Grande Romanzo dei Tempi del Cardinal Emanuel Madruzzo*

'Daddy, what's an optimist?' said Pat to Mike while they were walking down the street together one day. 'One who thought that M. Asquith wasn't going to write any more,' replied the absent-minded professor, as he wound up the cat and put the clock out. That gifted entertainer, the Countess of Oxford and Asquith, author of 'The Autobiography of Margot Asquith' (four volumes, ready boxed, suitable for throwing purposes), reverts to tripe in a new book deftly entitled 'Lay Sermons'. I think it must be pleasanter to be M. Asquith than to be any other living human being...

In this book of essays, which has all the depth and glitter of a worn dime, the Countess walks right up to such subjects as Health, Human Nature, Fame, Character, Marriage, Politics, and Opportunities. A rather large order, you might say, but it leaves the lady with unturned hair. Successively, she knocks down and drags out each topic. And there is something vastly stirring in the way in which, no matter where she takes off from, she brings the discourse back to Margot Asquith. Such singleness of purpose is met but infrequently...

The affair between M. Asquith and M. Asquith will live as one of the prettiest love stories in all history.

Dorothy Parker on *Lay Sermons* by Margot Asquith, in the *New Yorker*

A combination of Little Nell and Lady Macbeth.

Alexander Woollcott on Dorothy Parker

'That's a very good idea, Piglet,' said Pooh. 'We'll practise it now as we go along. But it's no good going home to practise it, because it's a special Outdoor Song Which Has To Be Sung In The Snow.'

'Are you sure?' asked Piglet anxiously.

'Well, you'll see, Piglet, when you listen. Because this is how it begins. The more it Snows-tiddely-pom —'

'Tiddely what?' said Piglet.

(He took, as you might say, the words out of your correspondent's mouth.)

'Pom!' said Pooh. 'I put it in to make it hummy.'

And it is that word 'hummy', my darlings, that marks the first place in 'The House at Pooh Corner' at which Tonstant Weader Fwowed up.

Dorothy Parker on *The House at Pooh Corner* by A. A. Milne, 'Constant Reader' review in the *New Yorker*

Oh for the hour of Herod.

Anthony Hope Hawkins on *Peter Pan* by J. M. Barrie

The triumph of sugar over diabetes.

George Jean Nathan on the works of J. M. Barrie

Nothing but a pack of lies.

Damon Runyon on *Alice in Wonderland* by Lewis Carroll

Almost pure gingerbread. It has bite, a certain flavour, but it turns into a gluey mass when chewed.

San Francisco Examiner on *Notes from a Bottle Found on the Beach at Carmel* by Evan Connell

From the moment I picked up your book until I laid it down I was convulsed with laughter. Someday I intend reading it.

Groucho Marx on *Dawn Ginsbergh's Revenge* by Sidney J. Perelman

The long experience of the book, personally speaking, was like a long hike home in wet socks and gym shoes, uncomfortable and unnecessary.

Out on May Sarton

I think her lack of greater popularity is due to her habit of dissecting her bowels and displaying for public observation.
Maine Life on May Sarton

Insects sting, not from malice, but because they want to live. It is the same with critics – they desire our blood, not our pain.
Friedrich Nietzsche

Show me a critic without prejudices, and I'll show you an arrested cretin.
George Jean Nathan

A reviewer is obligated to point out typographical errors, no matter how trivial. In the 'About the Author' note at the end of the book, we are told 'Roy Blount, Jr is a novelist. Now.' This makes sense only if the errant 'w' at the end of the last word is omitted. Apart from this bit of inadvertent humour, *First Hubby* is flawlessly lame.
L. S. Klepp on *First Hubby* by Roy Blount, Jr., in *Entertainment Weekly*

The covers of this book are too far apart.
Ambrose Bierce, review

Asking a working writer what he thinks about critics is like asking a lamppost what he feels about dogs.
Christopher Hampton

Heath does not mention the Sahara. Anyone familiar with that desert will know about the Erg. The Erg is a high inland plateau, intensely dry, hot and shingly, more or less inimical to any form of life. The fact that the author's initials are E. R. G. proved fatally intrusive on my powers of free association, and the analogy ... offered irresistible proof that *le style c'est l'homme.* That this wretched, drivelling affair, its impressions fuzzy with jet lag and neutral-flavoured as an airline meal, should have been made into a best seller, with all the attendant flimflam of the hired train and 8.2 autographed copies per minute, is a signpost towards the gap between those who buy books and those who read them.

Jonathan Keats on *Travels* by Edward Heath in the *New Statesman*

The ratio of literacy to illiteracy is constant, but nowadays the illiterates can read and write.

Alberto Moravia

Read over your compositions, and wherever you meet with a passage which you think is particularly fine, strike it out.

Samuel Johnson, recalling the advice of a college tutor

A vain, silly, transparent coxcomb without either solid talents or a solid nature.

J. G. Lockhart on Samuel Pepys

There is a certain race of men that either imagine it their duty, or make it their amusement, to hinder the reception of every work of learning or genius, who stand as sentinels in the avenues of fame, and value themselves upon giving Ignorance and Envy the first notice of a prey.

Samuel Johnson, *Rambler*

It is only fair to Allen Ginsberg to remark on the utter lack of decorum of any kind in his dreadful little volume. *Howl* is meant to be a noun, but I can't help taking it as an imperative.

John Hollander on *Howl* by Allen Ginsberg, in the *Partisan Review*

Our American professors like their literature clear and cold
and pure and very dead.
Sinclair Lewis on receiving the Nobel Prize

The face that lunched a thousand shits.
Anonymous, of Aristotle Stassinopoulos's conviviality

So boring you fall asleep halfway through her name.
Alan Bennett on Arianna Stassinopoulos, in the *Observer*

I fell asleep reading a dull book, and I dreamed that I was
reading on, so I awoke from sheer boredom.
Heinrich Heine

He is not really a writer, but a non-stop talker to whom
someone has given a typewriter.
Gerald Brenan on Henry Miller, *Thoughts in a Dry Season*

A collection of short stories is generally thought to be a
horrendous clinker; an enforced courtesy for the elderly writer
who wants to display the trophies of his youth, along with his
trout flies.
John Cheever on short stories

Then there is my noble and biographical friend who has added
a new terror to death.
Sir Charles Wetherell, lawyer and judge, on Lord Campbell's *Lives of the Lord
Chancellors*. The quote is also attributed to John Lyndhurst, who was excluded
from the book because he was still alive

Mr Waugh, I always feel, is an antique in search of a period,
a snob in search of a class, perhaps even a mystic in search of
a beatific vision.
Malcolm Muggeridge on Evelyn Waugh

Beckett was early commandeered by Enthusiasts whose object is always to quarantine their heroes. Under their influence, critics dwindle into a priesthood, readers vanish into a congregation, and art freezes into a sacrament that can never be questioned.

Robert Robinson on Samuel Beckett's enthusiasts

I love it when you talk like that. It reminds me of how much we lost when the grammar schools went comprehensive.

Ann Leslie on Robert Robinson, who had been talking for some time

Sir Walter Scott, when all is said and done, is an inspired butler.

William Hazlitt

Hardy became a sort of village atheist brooding and blaspheming over the village idiot.

G. K. Chesterton on Thomas Hardy

Where were you fellows when the paper was blank?

Fred Allen to writers who heavily edited one of his scripts

My Lord

February 1755

I have been lately informed by the proprietor of The World that two papers in which my dictionary is recommended to the Public were written by your Lordship. To be so distinguished is an honour which, being very little accustomed to favours from the Great, I know not well how to receive, or in what terms to acknowledge.

When upon some slight encouragement I first visited your Lordship I was overpowered like the rest of Mankind by the enchantment of your address, and could not forbear to wish that I might boast myself Le Vainqueur du Vainqueur de la Terre, that I might obtain that regard for which I saw the world contending, but I found my attendance so little encouraged, that neither pride nor modesty would suffer me to continue it. When I had once addressed your Lordship in public, I had exhausted all the art of pleasing which a retired and uncourtly Scholar can possess. I had done all that I could, and no Man is well pleased to have his all neglected, be it ever so little.

Seven years, My Lord, have now passed since I waited in your outward Rooms or was repulsed from your Door, during which time I have been pushing on my work through difficulties of which it is useless to complain, and have brought it at last to the verge of Publication without one Act of assistance, one word of encouragement, or one smile of favour. Such treatment I did not expect, for I never had a Patron before . . .

Is not a Patron, My Lord, one who looks with unconcern on a Man struggling for Life in the water and when he has reached ground encumbers him with help? The notice which you have been pleased to take of my Labours, had it been early, had been kind; but it has been delayed till I am indifferent and cannot enjoy it, till I am solitary and cannot impart it, till I am known and do not want it.

I hope it is no very cynical asperity not to confess obligation where no benefit has been received, or to be unwilling that the Public should consider me as owing that to a Patron, which Providence has enabled me to do for myself.

Having carried on my work thus far with so little obligation to any Favourer of Learning I shall not be disappointed though

I should conclude it, if less be possible, with less, for I have been long wakened from that Dream of hope, in which I once boasted myself with so much exaltation, My lord, Your Lordship's Most humble Obedient Servant,
Sam: Johnson
Samuel Johnson to Lord Chesterfield

PATRON: n.s. One who countenances, supports or protects. Commonly a wretch who supports with insolence, and is paid with flattery.
Samuel Johnson, *Dictionary of the English Language*

They teach the morals of a whore, and the manners of a dancing master.
Samuel Johnson on Lord Chesterfield's letters

Very nice, though there are dull stretches.
Antoine de Rivarol on a two-line poem

Mentula conatur Pipleium scandere montem:
Musae furcillis praecipitem eiciunt.
[Mr Prick is trying to climb up the mount of poetry;
the Muses push him out head first with their pitchforks.]
Catullus, CV, on Mamurra's literary efforts, tr. Amy Richlin

Chaucer, notwithstanding the praises bestowed upon him, I think obscene and contemptible; he owes his celebrity merely to his antiquity.
Lord Byron on Geoffrey Chaucer. Attrib.

A hyena that wrote poetry in tombs.
Friedrich Nietzsche on Dante

A Methodist parson in Bedlam.
Horace Walpole on Dante

Dr Donne's verses are like the Peace of God, for they pass all understanding.
James I on John Donne

Malt does more than Milton can
To justify God's ways to man.
A. E. Housman, *A Shropshire Lad*, 'The Welsh Marches'

Our language sunk under him.
Joseph Addison on John Milton

The whole of Milton's poem, *Paradise Lost*, is such barbarous trash, so outrageously offensive to reason and to common sense that one is naturally led to wonder how it can have been tolerated by a people amongst whom astronomy, navigation and chemistry are understood.
William Cobbett on John Milton

Having never had any mental vision, he has now lost his bodily sight; a silly coxcomb, fancifying himself a beauty; an unclean beast, with nothing more human about him than his guttering eyelids; the fittest doom for him would be to hang him on the highest gallows, and set his head on the Tower of London.
Salmasius [Claude de Saumaise] on John Milton

Thomas Gray walks as if he had fouled his small-clothes and looks as if he smelt it.
Christopher Smart

There are two ways of disliking poetry. One is to dislike it. The other is to read Pope.

Oscar Wilde on Alexander Pope

The Phrenzy of the 'Poems' was bad enough in its way; but it did not alarm us half so seriously as the calm, settled, imperturbable drivelling idiocy of 'Endymion' ... Mr Hunt is a small poet, but he is a clever man. Mr Keats is a still smaller poet, and he is only a boy of pretty abilities, which he has done everything in his power to spoil ... We venture to make one small prophecy, that his bookseller will not a second time venture £50 upon any thing he can write. It is a better and a wiser thing to be a starved apothecary than a starved poet; so back to the shop, Mr John, back to 'plasters, pills, and ointment boxes', etc. But for Heaven's sake, young Sangrado, be a little more sparing of extenuatives and soporifics in your practice than you have been with your poetry.

Blackwood's review of *Endymion* by John Keats, probably written by John Gibson Lockhart with help from Christopher North

Here are Jonny Keats' piss-a-bed poetry, and three novels by God knows whom ... No more Keats, I entreat: flay him alive; if some of you don't I must skin him myself: there is no bearing the drivelling idiotism of the Mankin.

Lord Byron on John Keats

Fricassee of dead dog ... A truly unwise little book. The kind of man that Keats was gets ever more horrible to me. Force of hunger for pleasure of every kind, and want of all other force − such a soul, it would once have been very evident, was a chosen 'vessel of Hell'; and truly, for ever there is justice in that feeling.

Thomas Carlyle on Monckton Milnes's *Life of Keats*

Such writing is a sort of mental masturbation ... a bedlam vision produced by raw pork and opium.

Lord Byron on John Keats, letter to John Murray

A tadpole of the Lakes.

Lord Byron on John Keats

A denaturalized being who, having exhausted every species of sensual gratification, and drained the cup of sin to its bitterest dregs, is resolved to show that he is no longer human, even in his frailties, but a cool, unconcerned fiend.

John Styles on Lord Byron

Mad, bad, and dangerous to know.

Lady Caroline Lamb of Lord Byron

A man must serve his time to every trade
Save censure – critics all are ready made.

Lord Byron, *English Bards and Scotch Reviewers*

Byron! – he would be all forgotten today if he had lived to be a florid old gentleman with iron-grey whiskers, writing very long, very able letters to the *Times* about the Repeal of the Corn Laws.

Max Beerbohm on Lord Byron

It was to me offensive, and I can never make out his great power, which his admirers talk of. Why, a line of Wordsworth's

is a lever to lift the immortal spirit! Byron can only bore the spleen.
Charles Lamb on Lord Byron

Charles Lamb I sincerely believe to be in some considerable degree insane. A more pitiful, rickety, gasping, staggering, stammering tomfool I do not know.
Thomas Carlyle. Attrib.

Here is Miss Seward with six tomes of the most disgusting trash, sailing over Styx with a Foolscap over her periwig as complacent as can be – Of all Bitches dead or alive a scribbling woman is the most canine.
Lord Byron on Anna Seward

From the poetry of Lord Byron they drew a system of ethics compounded of misanthropy and voluptuousness – a system in which the two greatest commandments were to hate your neighbour and to love your neighbour's wife.
Thomas Babington Macaulay

His writing bears the same relation to poetry which a Turkey carpet bears to a picture. There are colours in the Turkey carpet out of which a picture might be made. There are words in Mr Montgomery's writing which, when disposed in certain orders and combinations, have made, and will make again, good poetry. But, as they now stand, they seem to be put together on principle in such a manner as to give no image of anything 'in the heavens above, or in the earth beneath, or in the waters under the earth'.
Thomas Babington Macaulay on Robert Montgomery

Shelley is a poor creature, who has said or done nothing worth a serious man being at the trouble of remembering ... Poor soul, he has always seemed to me an extremely weak creature; a poor, thin, spasmodic, hectic, shrill and pallid being ... The very voice of him, shrill, shrieky, to my ear has too much of the ghost.

Thomas Carlyle on Percy Bysshe Shelley

A lewd vegetarian.

Charles Kingsley on Percy Bysshe Shelley

A mere sodomite and a perfect leper.

Ralph Waldo Emerson on Algernon Swinburne

A foul mouth is so ill-matched with a white beard that I would gladly believe the newspaper-scribes alone responsible for the bestial utterances which they declare to have dropped from a teacher whom such disciples as these exhibit to our disgust and compassion as performing on their obscene platform the last tricks of tongue now possible to a gap-toothed and hoary ape, carried at first notice on the shoulder of [Thomas] Carlyle, and who now in his dotage spits and chatters from a dirtier perch of his finding and fouling: coryphaeus or choragus of his Bulgarian tribe of auto-coprophagous baboons, who make the filth they feed on.

Algernon Swinburne on Ralph Waldo Emerson

Sitting in a sewer, and adding to it.

Thomas Carlyle on Algernon Swinburne

Walt Whitman is as unacquainted with art as a hog with mathematics.

London Critic on Walt Whitman

Longfellow is to poetry what the barrel-organ is to music.
Van Wyck Brooks on Henry Wadsworth Longfellow

The gentleman was a sweet, beautiful soul, but I have entirely forgotten his name.
Ralph Waldo Emerson, attending Henry Wadsworth Longfellow's funeral

The word 'honor' in the mouth of Mr Webster is like the word 'love' in the mouth of a whore.
Ralph Waldo Emerson on Daniel Webster

Waldo is one of those people who would be enormously improved by death.
Saki, 'The Feast of Nemesis'

Two voices there are: one is of the deep;
It learns the storm-cloud's thunderous melody . . .
And one is of an old half-witted sheep
Which bleats articulate monotony . . .
And, Wordsworth, both are thine.
James Kenneth Stephen on William Wordsworth

He keeps one eye on a daffodil and the other on a canal-share.
Walter Savage Landor on William Wordsworth

Wordsworth went to the Lakes, but he never was a lake poet. He found in stones the sermons he had already put there.
Oscar Wilde on William Wordsworth

It is no more than moderately good. I put by its side the poems of Matthew Arnold and think what a delightfully loud splash the two would make if I dropped them into a river.
Dylan Thomas on the Immortality Ode by William Wordsworth

A weak, diffusive, weltering, ineffectual man . . . a great possibility that has not realized itself. Never did I see such apparatus got ready for thinking, and so little thought. He mounts scaffolding, pulleys, and tackle, gathers all the tools in the neighbourhood with labour, with noise, demonstration, precept, abuse, and sets – three bricks.

Thomas Carlyle on Samuel Taylor Coleridge

Carlyle is a poet to whom nature has denied the faculty of verse.

Alfred, Lord Tennyson on Thomas Carlyle, letter to Gladstone

English Literature's performing flea.

Sean O'Casey on P. G. Wodehouse

There is no setting the point of precedency between a louse and a flea.

Samuel Johnson on Christopher Smart, comparing him to Samuel Derrick

There was little about melancholia that he didn't know; there was little else that he did.

W. H. Auden on Alfred, Lord Tennyson

A fly would break its legs walking across his face.

Anonymous on W. H. Auden

My face looks like a wedding cake that has been left out in the rain.

W. H. Auden on himself

No poet or novelist wishes he were the only one who ever lived, but most of them wish they were the only one alive,

and quite a number fondly believe their wish has been granted.
W. H. Auden

An unmanly sort of man whose love-life seems to have been
largely confined to crying in laps and playing mouse.
W. H. Auden on Edgar Allan Poe

The higher water mark, so to speak, of Socialist literature is
W. H. Auden, a sort of gutless Kipling.
George Orwell, *The Road to Wigan Pier*

By appointment: Teddy Bear to the Nation.
Alan Bell on John Betjeman, in *The Times*

All right, then, I'll say it: Dante makes me sick.
Lope Félix de Vega Carpio after being told he was about to die

The finest collection of frames I ever saw.
Sir Humphry Davy, when asked what he thought of the Paris art galleries.
Attrib.

If people only knew as much about painting as I do, they
would never buy my pictures.
Sir Edwin Henry Landseer to W. P. Frith

If the old masters had labelled their fruit, one wouldn't be so
likely to mistake pears for turnips.
Mark Twain

If Botticelli were alive today he'd be working for *Vogue*.
Peter Ustinov

He bores me. He ought to have stuck to his flying machines.
Auguste Renoir on Leonardo da Vinci

Degas is nothing but a peeping Tom, behind the coulisses, and among the dressing-rooms of the ballet dancers, noting only the travesties on fallen debased womanhood.
Pamphlet published by the *Churchman*

The English public takes no interest in a work of art until it is told that the work in question is immoral.
Oscar Wilde

I never saw anything so impudent on the walls of any exhibition, in any country, as last year in London. It was a daub professing to be a 'harmony in pink and white' (or some such nonsense); absolute rubbish, and which had taken about a quarter of an hour to scrawl or daub – it had no pretence to be called a painting. The price asked for it was two hundred and fifty guineas.
John Ruskin on James Whistler's *Symphony in Grey and Green*

I doubt that art needed Ruskin any more than a moving train needs one of its passengers to shove it.
Tom Stoppard on John Ruskin, in *The Times Literary Supplement*

A life passed among pictures does not make a painter – else the policeman in the National Gallery might assert himself, as well as allege, that he who lives in a library must needs die a poet. Let not Mr Ruskin flatter himself that more education makes the difference between himself and the policeman when both stand gazing in the Gallery. There they might remain till the end of time; the one decently silent, the other saying, in good English, many high-sounding empty things, like the crackling of thorns under a poet – undismayed by the presence of the Masters with whose names he is sacrilegiously familiar; whose intentions he interprets, whose vices he discovers with the facility of the incapable, and whose virtues he descants upon with a verbosity and flow of language that would, could we hear it, give Titian the same shock of surprise that was Balaam's when the first great critic proffered his opinion.

James Whistler on John Ruskin, *The Gentle Art of Making Enemies*

That he is indeed one of the very greatest masters of painting, is my opinion. And I may add that in this opinion Mr Whistler himself entirely concurs.

Oscar Wilde on James Whistler

A LADY: I only know of two painters in the world: yourself and Velasquez.
WHISTLER: Why drag in Velasquez?

James Whistler

I don't mind. I have gloves on.

Mark Twain after running his hand over a Whistler painting, which caused the artist to exclaim: 'Don't touch that. Can't you see, it isn't dry yet.'

Well, not bad, but there are decidedly too many of them, and they are not very well arranged. I would have done it differently.

James Whistler when asked if he agreed that the stars were especially beautiful one night

Perhaps not, but then you can't call yourself a great work of nature.

James Whistler after a sitter complained that his portrait was not a great work of art.

Maybe, my dear, but the shock will come when you see what you paint.

James Whistler to a student who told him that she only painted what she saw

The explanation is quite simple. I wished to be near my mother.

James Whistler after a snob asked him why he had been born in such an unfashionable place as Lowell, Massachusetts

I cannot tell you that, madam. Heaven has granted me no offspring.

James Whistler when asked if he thought genius hereditary

Mr Whistler has always spelt art with a capital 'I'.

Oscar Wilde on James Whistler

GENTLEMEN –
. . . What has Oscar in common with Art? except that he dines at our tables and picks from our platters the plums for the pudding he peddles in the provinces. Oscar – the amiable, irresponsible, esurient Oscar – with no more sense of a picture than of the fit of a coat, has the courage of the opinions . . . of others!
With . . . Oscar you have avenged the Academy.
    I am, Gentlemen, yours obediently.
    JAMES McNEILL WHISTLER.

James Whistler on Oscar Wilde, letter to the committee of the National Art Exhibition in the *World*

With our James vulgarity begins at home, and should be allowed to stay there.

Oscar Wilde on James Whistler, letter to the *World*

Art

A poor thing, Oscar! – but, for once, I suppose your own.
James Whistler on Oscar Wilde

As for borrowing Mr Whistler's ideas about art, the only thoroughly original ideas I have ever heard him express have had reference to his own superiority as a painter over painters greater than himself.
Oscar Wilde on James Whistler, letter, in *Truth*

... I am awe-stricken and tremble, for truly, 'the rage of the sheep is terrible!'
James Whistler on Oscar Wilde, letter, in *Truth*

I have been to it and am pleased to find it more odious than I even dared to hope.
Samuel Butler on the Rossetti Exhibition

A pot of paint has been thrown in the public's face.
Variously believed to have been said by John Ruskin about Whistler's painting *Nocturne in Black and Gold: The Falling Rocker*, or by Camille Mauclair about Jean Puy's painting *Stroll under the Pines*

It resembles a tortoise-shell cat having a fit in a plate of tomatoes.
Mark Twain on J. M. W. Turner's *The Slave Ship*

It makes me look as if I was straining a stool.
Winston Churchill on his portrait by Graham Sutherland

If my husband would ever meet a woman on the street who looked like the women in his paintings, he would fall over in a dead faint.
Mrs Pablo Picasso on her husband's paintings

His pictures seem to resemble, not pictures, but a sample book of patterns of linoleum.
Cyril Asquith on Paul Klee

The only genius with an IQ of 60.
Gore Vidal on Andy Warhol

Epstein is a great sculptor. I wish he would wash.
Ezra Pound on Jacob Epstein

How can I take an interest in my work when I don't like it?
Francis Bacon

I stick to my business, which is art. Suggest you stick to yours, which is butchery.
Jacob Epstein, telegram to Nikita Khrushchev after he visited Britain in the 1950s and made what was described as a 'vigorous' observation about the Epstein sculpture in New College Chapel

The immoral profession of musical criticism must be abolished.
Richard Wagner

Of all the bulls that live, this hath the greatest ass's ears.
Elizabeth I on the musician John Bull

Those people on the stage are making such a noise I can't hear a word you're saying.
Henry Taylor Parker, American music critic, rebuking some members of an audience who were talking near him

I like Wagner's music better than any other music. It is so loud that one can talk the whole time without people hearing what one says. That is a great advantage.
Oscar Wilde on Richard Wagner

I love Wagner, but the music I prefer is that of a cat hung up by its tail outside a window and trying to stick to the panes of glass with its claws.
Charles Baudelaire on Richard Wagner

Wagner has beautiful moments but awful quarter hours.
Gioacchino Rossini on Richard Wagner

The music of Wagner imposes mental tortures that only algebra has a right to inflict.
Paul de Saint-Victor on Richard Wagner, in *La Presse*

It has no more real pretension to be called music than the jangling and clashing of gongs and other uneuphonious instruments with which the Chinamen, on the brow of a hill, fondly thought to scare away our English blue-jackets.
The *Musical World* on Richard Wagner's *Lohengrin*

Is Wagner a human being at all? Is he not rather a disease?
Friedrich Nietzsche on Richard Wagner

The wild Wagnerian corybantic orgy, this din of brasses, tin pans and kettles, this Chinese or Caribbean clatter with wood sticks and ear-cutting scalping knives ... Heartless sterility, obliteration of all melody, all tonal charm, all music ... This revelling in the destruction of all tonal essence, raging satanic fury in the orchestra, this diabolic, lewd caterwauling, scandal-mongering, gun-toting music, with an orchestral accompaniment slapping you in the face ...
J. L. Klein on Richard Wagner

I like your Opera. One day I think I'll set it to music.

Richard Wagner to a young composer; also attributed to Ludwig van Beethoven

After Rossini dies, who will there be to promote his music?

Richard Wagner on Gioacchino Rossini

Don't trouble yourself to play further. I much prefer the second.

Gioacchino Rossini to a would-be composer who had just played the first of two works from which he wished Rossini to choose the better

Rossini would have been a great composer if his teacher had spanked him enough on the backside.

Ludwig van Beethoven on Gioacchino Rossini

What can you do with it? It's like a lot of yaks jumping about.

Sir Thomas Beecham on the Seventh Symphony by Ludwig van Beethoven

When I composed that, I was conscious of being inspired by God Almighty. Do you think I can consider your puny little fiddle when He speaks to me?

Ludwig van Beethoven in reply to a complaint by a violinist that a passage was unplayable

All Bach's last movements are like the running of a sewing-machine.

Arnold Bax on Johann Sebastian Bach

The audience seemed rather disappointed; they expected the ocean, something big, something colossal, but they were served instead with some agitated water in a saucer.

Louis Schneider on *La Mer* by Claude Debussy

I liked the bit about quarter to eleven.

Erik Satie on 'From Dawn to Noon on the Sea' from *La Mer* by Claude Debussy

Very vile – a catarrhal or sternutatory concerto. One frequently recurring phrase is a graphic instrumentation of a fortissimo sneeze, and a long passage is evidently meant to suggest a protracted, agonized bravura on the pocket handkerchief.

George Templeton Strong on a concerto by Franz Liszt, *Diary*

Liszt's orchestral music is an insult to art. It is gaudy musical harlotry, savage and incoherent bellowings.

Boston Gazette on Franz Liszt

The leader of cacophonists ... is Arnold Schoenberg ... He learned a lesson from militant suffragettes. He was ignored till he began to smash the parlor furniture, throw bombs, and hitch together ten pianolas, all playing different tunes, whereupon everybody began to talk about him. In Schoenberg's later works, all the laws of construction, observed by the masters, from Bach to Wagner, are ignored, insulted, trampled upon. The statue of Venus, the Goddess of Beauty, is knocked from its pedestal and replaced by the stone image of the Goddess of Ugliness, with the hideous features of a Hottentot hag.

Henry T. Finck, *Musical Progress*

Shostakovich is without doubt the foremost composer of pornographic music in the history of art. He has accomplished the feat of penning passages which, in their faithful portrayal of what is going on, become obscene ... The whole scene is little better than a glorification of the sort of stuff that filthy pencils write on lavatory walls.

W. J. Henderson on Dmitri Shostakovich, in the New York *Sun*

I had another dream the other day about music critics. They were small and rodent-like with padlocked ears, as if they had stepped out of a painting by Goya.

Igor Stravinsky, in the *Evening Standard*

Rachmaninov's immortalizing totality was his scowl. He was a six-and-a-half-foot-tall scowl.

Igor Stravinsky on Sergei Rachmaninov

I can compare *Le Carnaval Romain* by Berlioz to nothing but the caperings and gibberings of a big baboon, over-excited by a dose of alcoholic stimulus.

George Templeton Strong on Hector Berlioz, *Diary*

The opening Allegro took me straight back to childhood and gave me in turn the rusty windlass of a well, the interlinking noises of a goods train that is being shunted, then the belly-rumblings of a little boy acutely ill after a raid on an orchard, and finally the singular alarmed noise of poultry being worried to death by a Scotch terrier. The second movement gave me continuously and throughout its short length the noise of a November wind in telegraph poles on a lonely country road. The third movement began with a dog howling at midnight, proceeded to imitate the regurgitations of the less-refined or lower-middle-class type of water-closet cistern, modulating thence into the mass snoring of a naval dormitory around dawn – and concluded inconsequentially with the cello reproducing the screech of an ungreased wheelbarrow. The fourth movement reminded me immediately and persistently and vividly of something I have never thought of since the only time I heard it: the noise of a Zulu village in the Glasgow Exhibition – a hubbub all the more singular, because it had a background of skirling Highland bagpipes. Both noises emerged in this final movement of this Fourth Quartet of Béla Bartók.

Alan Dent on Béla Bartók, quoted in *The Later Ego* by James Agate

In the first movement alone I took notice of six pregnancies and at least four miscarriages.

Sir Thomas Beecham on the Seventh Symphony by Anton Bruckner

To me it seems quite obvious that the real Brahms is nothing more than a sentimental voluptuary ... He is the most wanton of composers ... Only his wantonness is not vicious; it is that of a great baby ... rather tiresomely addicted to dressing himself up as Handel or Beethoven and making a prolonged and intolerable noise.

George Bernard Shaw on Johannes Brahms, in the *World*

If there is anyone here whom I have not insulted, I beg his pardon.

Johannes Brahms on leaving a gathering of friends

Brahms is just like Tennyson, an extraordinary musician with the brains of a third-rate village policeman.

George Bernard Shaw on Johannes Brahms

I played over the music of that scoundrel Brahms. What a giftless bastard! It annoys me that this self-inflated mediocrity is hailed as a genius. Why, in comparison with him, Raff is a giant, not to speak of Rubinstein, who is after all a live and important human being, while Brahms is chaotic and absolutely empty dried-up stuff.

Peter Tchaikovsky on Johannes Brahms, *Diary*

Music that stinks to the ear.

Eduard Hanslick on Peter Tchaikovsky

Splitting the convulsively inflated larynx of the Muse, Berg utters tortured mistuned cackling, a pandemonium of chopped-up orchestral sounds, mishandled men's throats, bestial outcries, bellowing, rattling, and all other evil noises ... Berg is the poisoner of the well of German music.

Berlin *Germania* on Alban Berg

Here love has nothing in it but filth, dirt, cold cruelty and sticky frog-like sexuality, combined with the dry rationalism of a biped calculating machine.

V. Gorodinsky on Ernst Křenek, *Music of Spiritual Poverty*

It sounded like as though a pack of rats were being slowly tortured to death, while, from time to time, a dying cow moaned.

Berlin *Signale* on *Dichotomy* by Wallingford Riegger

The musical equivalent of blancmange.

Bernard Levin on Frederick Delius

Listening to the Fifth Symphony of Ralph Vaughan Williams is like staring at a cow for forty-five minutes.

Aaron Copland

Critics are misbegotten abortions.

Ralph Vaughan Williams on music critics

Music

....

I can say nothing for the music of *Madame Butterfly*. Western music is too complicated for a Japanese. Even Caruso's celebrated singing does not appeal very much more than the barking of a dog in faraway woods.

Jihei Hashigushi after attending the New York première of *Madame Butterfly* by Puccini

You know whatta you do when you shit? Singing, it's the same thing, only up!

Enrico Caruso

It is quite untrue that the English people don't appreciate music. They may not understand it but they absolutely love the noise it makes.

Sir Thomas Beecham

I had not realized that the Arabs were so musical.

Sir Thomas Beecham on hearing that a concert by Malcolm Sargent in Tel Aviv had been interrupted by the sound of gunfire directed at the concert hall

A kind of musical by Malcolm Sargent.

Sir Thomas Beecham on Herbert von Karajan

The musical equivalent of St Pancras station.

Sir Thomas Beecham on Edward Elgar's Symphony in A Flat

A glorified bandmaster.

Sir Thomas Beecham on Arturo Toscanini

Madame, there you sit with that magnificent instrument between your legs, and all you can do is *scratch* it!

Arturo Toscanini to a woman cellist; also attributed to Sir Thomas Beecham

CELLIST: What shall I do next?

SIR THOMAS BEECHAM: Get married.

Sir Thomas Beecham to a young female cellist at an audition, after she had completed the first movement of a concerto

If you will make a point of singing 'All we, like sheep, have gone astray' with a little less satisfaction, we shall meet the aesthetical as well as the theological requirements.

Sir Thomas Beecham to a choir

Brass bands are all very well in their place – outdoors and several miles away.

Sir Thomas Beecham. Attrib.

Thank you, and now would you pull the chain.

Sir Thomas Beecham to an incompetent tuba player

There are two golden rules for an orchestra: start together and finish together. The public doesn't give a damn what goes on in between.

Sir Thomas Beecham

A musicologist is a man who can read music but can't hear it.

Sir Thomas Beecham

Dominoes.

George Bernard Shaw to the conductor of a palm-court orchestra in a restaurant, who had asked Shaw if he would like to request the orchestra to play anything in particular

One should try everything once, except incest and folk-dancing.

Arnold Bax

When Jack Benny plays the violin, it sounds as if the strings are still back in the cat.
Fred Allen

George Melly your a repulsive sweaty faced lout singing love songs. Why your past it. Hang your gun up. And all your dirty jokes leave them to the real comedians. You have a mouth like a ducks ass. Have you only one suit and shabby at that. And your dirty suggestive songs. Somebody ought to tell you. You dirty minded oaf.

Your a load of rubbish.
Anonymous letter to George Melly. The spelling mistakes are reproduced from the original

His approach to the microphone is that of an accused man pleading with a hostile jury.
Kenneth Tynan on Frankie Lane

Miss Truman is a unique American phenomenon with a pleasant voice, of little size and fair quality ... There are few moments during her recital when one can relax and feel confident she will make her goal, which is the end of the song.
Paul Hume on the singer Margaret Truman, in the *Washington Post*

I have just read your lousy review buried in the back pages of the paper. You sound like a frustrated old man who never made a success, an eight-ulcer man on a four-ulcer job, and all four ulcers working. I have never met you, but if I do you'll need a new nose and plenty of beefsteak and perhaps a supporter below.
Harry S Truman replying to Paul Hume's review of his daughter (Margaret Truman), in the *Washington Post*

Sinatra could be terribly nice one minute and, well, not so nice the next. I was not impressed with the creeps and Mafia types he kept around him.
Prince Charles on Frank Sinatra

To hear Tom Jones sing Sinatra's *My Way* is roughly akin to watching Tab Hunter play King Lear. Mr Jones is, in the words of his own hit, not unusual ... at least not as a singer; as a sex symbol he is nothing short of inexplicable.
Sheridan Morley, in *Punch*

Do you gargle with pebbles?
Prince Philip to Tom Jones, after a Royal Variety Show

If white bread could sing it would sound like Olivia Newton-John.
Anonymous review

The Beatles are not merely awful, I would consider it sacrilegious to say anything less than that they are godawful. They are so unbelievably horrible, so appallingly unmusical, so dogmatically insensitive to the magic of the art, that they qualify as crowned heads of anti-music, even as the impostor popes went down in history as 'anti-popes'.
William F. Buckley, Jr.

Their lyrics are unrecognizable as the Queen's English.
Edward Heath on the Beatles

This man has child-bearing lips.
Joan Rivers on Mick Jagger

You have Van Gogh's ear for music.
Billy Wilder to Cliff Osmond. Attrib.

Wood Green shopping centre has been committed to vinyl.
The *New Musical Express* on the pop group Five Star

Five bowls of muesli looking for a spoon.
The *New Musical Express* on the pop group Yes

The 'Mode' make very dubious puffing noises as though they
were blowing up a paddling pool.
Smash Hits on Depeche Mode

He has an attractive voice and a highly unattractive bottom.
In his concert performances he now spends more time
wagging the latter than exercising the former, thereby con-
forming to the established pattern by which popular enter-
tainers fall prey to the delusion that the public loves them for
themselves, and not for their work.
Clive James on Rod Stewart

Her voice sounded like an eagle being goosed.
Ralph Novak on Yoko Ono, in *People*

Boy George is all England needs – another queen who can't
dress.
Joan Rivers

I remember when pop music meant jerking off to pictures of
Marc Bolan and duffing up Bay City Rollers' fans in lunch
breaks. Being 13 was never as vapid as this. If it had been, we
would all be traffic wardens by now.
Melody Maker on the pop group Bros

They are the Hollow Men. They are electronic lice.
Anthony Burgess on disc jockeys, in *Punch*

Bambi with testosterone.
Owen Gleiberman on Prince, in *Entertainment Weekly*

A vacuum with nipples.
Otto Preminger on Marilyn Monroe

A walking X-ray.
Oscar Levant on Audrey Hepburn

The face to lauch a thousand dredgers.
Jack de Manio on Glenda Jackson in *Women in Love*

Diana Rigg is built like a brick mausoleum with insufficient flying buttresses.
John Simon reviewing *Abelard and Heloise* by Ronald Millar

Mummy, what is that lady *for*?
Child at a matinée performance by Hermione Gingold

A very *old* 13.
Noël Coward, describing an actress who had just had a facelift

Mr Gielgud has the most meaningless legs imaginable.
Ivor Brown on John Gielgud's Romeo

His ears make him look like a taxi-cab with both doors open.
Howard Hughes on Clark Gable

If you say 'Hiya, Clark, how are you?' he's stuck for an answer.
Ava Gardner on Clark Gable

She was good at playing abstract confusion in the same way that a midget is good at being short ... As far as talent goes,

Marilyn Monroe was so minimally gifted as to be unemployable, and anyone who holds to the opinion that she was a great natural comic identifies himself immediately as a dunce.
Clive James

It's like kissing Hitler.
Tony Curtis on kissing Marilyn Monroe

I watched *The Music Lovers*. One can't really blame Tchaikovsky for preferring boys. Anyone might become a homosexualist who had once seen Glenda Jackson naked.
Auberon Waugh, in *Private Eye*

You have obviously spent so much time with your head wedged between your buttocks that your vision has been obscured by the reflection of your own putrid entrails. If the art of literary or dramatic criticism is to remain viable, we must seek to eliminate people like you who degrade the art form by taking cheap shots at performers' physical liabilities and who must darkly illuminate their critiques with pseudo-intellectual name calling. If you must persist in deriding Ms Minnelli's so-called imperfections, at least do so with the stroke of your pen rather than with the excrement of your bowels.
From a letter to John Simon, drama critic of *New York* magazine, after he had passed unfavourable comment on the facial appearance and acting ability of Liza Minnelli

The syphilis and gonorrhoea of the theatre.
David Mamet on Frank Rich and John Simon, critics

As wholesome as a bowl of cornflakes and at least as sexy.
Dwight MacDonald on Doris Day

Maybe it's the hair. Maybe it's the teeth. Maybe it's the intellect. No, it's the hair.
Tom Shales on Farrah Fawcett

A bargain basement Bette Davis, whose lightest touch as a comedienne would stun a horse.
Time on Susan Hayward

He looks as if his idea of fun would be to find a cold damp grave and sit in it.
Richard Winnington on Paul Henreid

She looked as though butter wouldn't melt in her mouth — or anywhere else.
Elsa Lanchester on Maureen O'Hara. Attrib.

A face unclouded by thought.
Lillian Hellman on Norma Shearer

[A] vamp who destroys families and sucks on husbands like a praying mantis.
Il Tempo on Elizabeth Taylor at the time of her affair with Richard Burton during the filming of *Cleopatra*

Overweight, overbosomed, overpaid and under-talented, she set the acting profession back a decade.
David Susskind on Elizabeth Taylor in *Cleopatra*

Miss Taylor is monotony in a slit skirt, a pre-Christian Elizabeth Arden with sequinned eyelids and occasions constantly too large for her.
New Statesman on Elizabeth Taylor in *Cleopatra*

Elizabeth Taylor looks like two small boys fighting underneath a mink blanket.

Blackwell, American designer

Just how garish her commonplace accent, squeakily shrill voice, and the childish petulance with which she delivers her lines are, my pen is neither scratchy nor leaky enough to convey.

John Simon on Elizabeth Taylor's Kate, *The Taming of the Shrew*

... An incipient double chin, legs too short, and she has a slight pot belly.

Richard Burton on Elizabeth Taylor

I will marry her ... Of course, you may be quite certain I shall be at the centre of the stage. Elizabeth will be in the wings – knitting.

Richard Burton on Elizabeth Taylor

Her arms are too fat, her legs are too short, and she is too big in the bust.

Richard Burton on Elizabeth Taylor, his new wife

In general, Mr Burton resembles a stuffed cabbage.

Harry Medved and Randy Dreyfuss on Richard Burton in *The Assassination of Trotsky, The Fifty Worst Films of All Time*

She cannot change her face, which is that of a worried hamster.

Review of Prunella Scales playing all six female parts in *Anatole France* by David Tylden-Wright

She looks like she combs her hair with an egg-beater.

Louella Parsons on Joan Collins

He looks like an extra in a crowd scene by Hieronymus Bosch.
Kenneth Tynan on Don Rickles, in the *New Yorker*

Like acting with two and a half tons of condemned veal.
Coral Browne on a leading man

When he mounts into the air it is by means of a chair and a table, and his descents are similarly accomplished.
James Agate on Fred Astaire in *The Gay Divorce*, in the *Sunday Times*

He has taken to ambling across our stages in a spectral, shell-shocked manner, choosing odd moments to jump and frisk, like a man through whom an electric current is being inter-mittently passed.
Kenneth Tynan on Ralph Richardson in *The White Carnation* by R. C. Sherriff

No man looking like a golliwog can persuade us that he is talking like a god.
Harold Hobson on Ralph Richardson as Othello

Tony Britton's habit of curling his lip villainously and so relentlessly gives one the impression that he has had it per-manently waved.
Plays and Players on Tony Britton in *A Woman of No Importance* by Oscar Wilde

A bore is starred.
Village Voice review of *A Star is Born* starring Barbra Streisand

She looks like a cross between an aardvark and an albino rat surmounted by a platinum-coated horse bun.
John Simon on Barbra Streisand

A woman whose face looked as if it had been made of sugar and someone had licked it.
George Bernard Shaw on Isadora Duncan

She not only worships the Golden Calf, she barbecues it for lunch.
Oscar Levant on Zsa Zsa Gabor

He has delusions of adequacy.
Walter Kerr on an actor

I've just spent an hour talking to Tallulah for a few minutes.
Fred Keating on Tallulah Bankhead

I thought I told you to wait in the car.
Tallulah Bankhead, when greeted by a former admirer after many years. Attrib.

She was always a star, but only intermittently a good actress.
Brendan Gill on Tallulah Bankhead, in *The Times*

She was an open, wayward, free, cosmopolitan, liberated, sensuous human being. In thus systematically invading her own privacy she was the first of the modern personalities.
Lee Israel on Tallulah Bankhead

I'm as pure as the driven slush.
Tallulah Bankhead

Dorothy [Tutin] played St Joan like a beatnik in a coffee-bar.
Alan Drury, in the *Listener*

Like a toastmaster celebrating his golden wedding.
James Agate on Henry Ainley as Prospero in *The Tempest*, in the *Sunday Times*

Julian Glover's Antony ... enters red, sweaty and with his bow-tie askew, like some raddled, over-used debs' delight.

Review of *Antony and Cleopatra*

Millamant must be the empress of her sex, and her words, whether tinkling like a fountain or cascading like Niagara, must always flow from a great height. From Miss Brown's mouth they do not flow at all; they leak ...

Kenneth Tynan on Pamela Brown in *The Way of the World* by William Congreve

Miss Moira Lister speaks all her lines as if they are written in very faint ink on a tele-printer slightly too far away to be read with comfort.

Bernard Levin reviewing *The Gazebo* by Alec Coppel

Denis Quilley played the role with all the charm and animation of the leg of a billiard table.

Bernard Levin on Denis Quilley as Charles Condamine in *High Spirits* (a musical version of Noël Coward's *Blithe Spirit*)

As swashbuckling Cyrano, Mr Woodward's performance buckles more than it swashes.

Kenneth Tynan on Edward Woodward in *Cyrano*, in the *Spectator*

We are privileged to see Mr Samuel Goldwyn's latest 'discovery'. All we can say about this actor is that he is tall, dark and not the slightest bit handsome.

Detroit Free Press on David Niven in *Dodsworth*

This was Doris Day's first picture; before she became a virgin.

Oscar Levant on Doris Day in *Romance on the High Seas*

Guido Nadzo was Nadzo Guido.
Brooks Atkinson on Valentino look-alike Guido Nadzo

Mr Creston Clarke played King Lear at the Tabor Grand last night. All through five acts of the Shakespearean tragedy he played the king as though under the premonition that someone was about to play the ace.
Eugene Field, Denver *Post*

Not content to stop the show, she merely slowed it down.
Anonymous, of Elaine Paige

It is a generous role for womanly and impassioned actresses, and many performers have essayed it. I can think of four, however, who have not: Totie Fields, W. C. Fields, Tut-ankhamen's mummy, and a trained monkey. Not until now, that is. Miss Gordon's performance combines elements of all four.
John Simon on Ruth Gordon in the title role of *Mrs Warren's Profession* by George Bernard Shaw

Very believably playing an English secretary, Julie fell for Omar, who had been cast as a Russian spy because there was no role available as a date-picker.
Clive James on Omar Sharif in *The Tamarind Seed* co-starring Julie Andrews, in the *Observer*

You thought Dirk Benedict had problems in TV's *Battlestar Galactica*? In *Scavenger Hunt*, he really had problems – in one mercifully brief scene, he was out-acted by a jock-strap.
Rona Barrett on Dirk Benedict

It is greatly to Mrs Patrick Campbell's credit that, bad as the play was, her acting was worse. It was a masterpiece of failure.
George Bernard Shaw on Mrs Patrick Campbell

When you were a little boy, somebody ought to have said 'hush' just once.
Mrs Patrick Campbell to George Bernard Shaw

She was a sinking ship firing upon her rescuers.
Alexander Woollcott on Mrs Patrick Campbell

Oh, to be in England, now that June's here.
Robert Garland about Lady June Inverclyde, who had just arrived in America

In real life, Keaton believes in God. But she also believes that the radio works because there are tiny people inside it.
Woody Allen on Diane Keaton

An acting style that's really a nervous breakdown in slow-motion.
John Simon on Diane Keaton

Do you know how they are going to decide the Shakespeare–Bacon dispute? They are going to dig up Shakespeare and dig up Bacon; they are going to set their coffins side by side, and they are going to get Tree to recite Hamlet to them. And the one who turns in his coffin will be the author of the play.
W. S. Gilbert on Herbert Beerbohm Tree

At the end, when the whale has lured Harris north with a come-hither flick of its tail, Miss Rampling is caught in the ice floes, leaping from one to t'other and clad in thigh boots, homespun poncho *and a turban*, as if she expected David Bailey

to surface and photograph her for *Vogue*'s Arctic number.
Alexander Walker on Charlotte Rampling in *Orca the Killer Whale*, in the
Evening Standard

Dame Anna Neagle was game enough to have a little stab at
the Charleston, and was wildly and sympathetically applauded
by admirers who plainly felt that any gesture more extravagant
than holding a hand above her head – as though hailing a cab,
or conceivably signalling for help – was a grave imposition
upon a Lady of her advanced years.
Kenneth Hurren reviewing *No, No, Nanette*, in the *Spectator*

Tallulah Bankhead barged down the Nile last night as Cleopatra – and sank.
John Mason Brown

A plumber's idea of Cleopatra.
W. C. Fields on Mae West

She has a face that belongs to the sea and the wind, with large
rocking-horse nostrils and teeth that you just know bite an
apple every day.
Cecil Beaton on Katharine Hepburn

Katharine Hepburn ran the whole gamut of emotions from
A to B.
Dorothy Parker reviewing *The Lake* by Dorothy Massingham and Murray
MacDonald

I think they have made a slight mistake. They've left the show
in Detroit, or wherever it was warming up, and brought in
the publicity stills.
Walter Kerr on the musical *Ilya Darling*

I have knocked everything but the knees of the chorus girls, and nature has anticipated me there.

Percy Hammond, critic, on a musical

Critics are ink-stained wretches.

Alexander Woollcott

Actors? They're poor, abject, disagreeable, perverse, ill-minded slightly malicious creatures. They must have the centre of the stage or at least the second-centre. They'd like to stop, but they can't. And of that august company of idiots, I'm afraid I'm a member.

Richard Burton

An actor's a guy who, if you ain't talking about him, ain't listening.

Marlon Brando

You can pick out actors by the glazed look that comes into their eyes when the conversation wanders away from themselves.

Michael Wilding

Actors should be treated like cattle.

Alfred Hitchcock

Directors are people too short to be actors.

Josh Greenfeld on film directors

He was once Slightly in *Peter Pan*, and has been wholly in Peter Pan ever since.

Kenneth Tynan on Noël Coward. Attrib.

He was his own greatest invention.
John Osborne on Noël Coward

If they'd stuffed the child's head up the horse's arse, they would have solved two problems at once.
Noël Coward, referring to a performance starring child actress Bonnie Langford and a horse after the latter defecated on stage

The reason why so many people turned up at Louis Mayer's funeral was because they wanted to make sure he was dead.
Sam Goldwyn

It proves what they always say: give the public what they want to see and they'll come out for it.
Anonymous, on the crowds at the funeral of Hollywood mogul Harry Cohn

What critics call dirty in our movies they call lusty in foreign films.
Billy Wilder

I'm sure pictures like this give people pimples.
Pauline Kael on *Sweet November*

Television? No good will come of this device. The word is half Greek and half Latin.
C. P. Scott

Television is a medium of entertainment which permits millions of people to listen to the same joke at the same time, and yet remain lonesome.
T. S. Eliot, in the *New York Post*

TV is an invention that permits you to be entertained in your living-room by people you wouldn't have in your home.
David Frost

There are days when any electrical appliance in the house, including the vacuum cleaner, seems to offer more entertainment possibilities than the TV set.
Harriet Van Horne

We are drowning our youngsters in violence, cynicism and sadism piped into the living-room and even the nursery. The grandchildren of the kids who used to weep because the Little Matchgirl froze to death now feel cheated if she isn't slugged, raped and thrown into a Bessemer converter.
Jenkin Lloyd Jones

I have beside me, as I write, two tubes of glutinous liquid, which, I am told, when mixed, will form an adhesive powerful enough to weld together two elephants who would rather part company, and hold up the Clifton Suspension Bridge should it ever run out of suspenders. I would prefer, however, to put this admirable concoction to a different use. I would like, in fact, to spoon out great dollops of it into your beard.
Letter to Elkan Allan, TV critic and compiler of 'Critical Viewer's Guide to the Week's Television' in the *Sunday Times*

I sometimes wonder which would be nicer – an opera without an interval, or an interval without an opera.
Ernest Newman

You know, I go to the theatre to be entertained ... I don't

want to see plays about rape, sodomy and drug addiction . . .
I can get all that at home.
Peter Cook, caption to cartoon in the *Observer*

Popular Stage-playes . . . are sinfull, heathenish, lewde,
ungodly Spectacles, and most pernicious Corruptions; condemned in all ages, as intolerable Mischiefes to Churches, to
Republickes, to the manners, mindes and soules of men. And
that the Profession of Play-poets, of Stage-players; together
with the penning, acting, and frequenting of Stage-playes, are
unlawful, infamous, and misbeseeming Christians.
William Prynne, seventeenth-century critic

A good many inconveniences attend play-going in any large
city, but the greatest of them is usually the play itself.
Kenneth Tynan

It had only one fault. It was kind of lousy.
James Thurber on a play

I saw it at a disadvantage – the curtain was up.
Walter Winchell on a show starring Earl Carroll

The play was a great success, but the audience was a disaster.
Oscar Wilde

Long experience has taught me that in England nobody goes
to the theatre unless he or she has bronchitis.
James Agate

Busy yourselves with that, you damned walruses, while the
rest of us proceed with the play.
John Barrymore, throwing a fish into the stalls of a coughing audience

I would just like to mention Robert Houdin who in the eighteenth century invented the vanishing bird-cage trick and the theatre matinée. May he rot and perish. Good afternoon.
Orson Welles, addressing the audience at the end of a matinée performance

It has taken 33 years for Jean-Paul Sartre's *The Devil and the Good Lord* to reach London, but our luck was bound to run out sooner or later.
Kenneth Hurren, in the *Mail on Sunday*

I've seen more excitement at the opening of an umbrella.
Earl Wilson, reviewing a play

All the joy of standing by at an autopsy.
Variety magazine on the film *Divorce His, Divorce Hers*

Watching my plays performed in London is like seeing them in translation.
Lillian Hellman

There was laughter at the back of the theatre, leading to the belief that someone was telling jokes back there.
George S. Kaufman on a Broadway comedy

Remarkable economy of means, and of effect.
Henry James on a Punch and Judy show

When Mr Wilbur calls his play *Halfway to Hell* he underestimates the distance.
Brooks Atkinson

Darling, they've absolutely ruined your perfectly dreadful play.
Tallulah Bankhead to Tennessee Williams after seeing the film version of *Orpheus Descending*, entitled *The Fugitive Kind*

A mishmash of Stalinism with New Dealism with Holly-woodism with opportunism with shaky experimentalism with mesmerism with onanism, all mosaicked into a remarkable portrait of what the makers of the film think the Soviet Union is like – a great glad two-million-dollar bowl of canned borscht, eminently approvable by the Institute of Good Housekeeping.

James Agee on *Mission to Moscow*

There is enough Irish comedy to make us wish Cromwell had done a more thorough job.

James Agee on *Fort Apache*

They only got two things right – the camels and the sand.

Lowell Thomas on *Lawrence of Arabia*

To sit through this film is something like holding an elephant on your lap for two hours and fifteen minutes.

Time on *Circus World*

As synthetic and padded as the transvestite's cleavage.

Frank Rich, 'The Butcher of Broadway', on *La Cage aux Folles*, in *The New York Times*

An American musical, so bad that at times I longed for the boy-meets-tractor theme of Soviet drama.

Bernard Levin on Rodgers and Hammerstein's *Flower Drum Song*, in the *Daily Express*

There is less in this than meets the eye.

Tallulah Bankhead on a revival of a play by Maeterlinck

He displayed a sneaky knack for extending the life of a

production beyond the reasonable expectations of the play-
wright's mother.
Walter Kerr on David Merrick

Very well then: I say Never.
George Jean Nathan on *Tonight or Never*

It can probably be said that Pinter raised to a new level of
acceptability the kind of play in which the audience not only
has no precise idea of what is going on, but seriously doubts
whether the author has, either.
Kenneth Hurren on *The Birthday Party* by Harold Pinter, in the *Mail on
Sunday*

Shakespeare, Madam, is obscene, and, thank God, we are
sufficiently advanced to have found it out.
Frances Trollope on William Shakespeare

One of the greatest geniuses that ever existed, Shakespeare
undoubtedly wanted taste.
Horace Walpole on William Shakespeare

We can say of Shakespeare, that never has a man turned so
little knowledge to such great account.
T. S. Eliot on William Shakespeare

Not a single one [of the sonnets] is very admirable ... They
are hot and pothery: there is much condensation, little
delicacy; like raspberry jam without cream, without crust,
without bread.
Walter Savage Landor on William Shakespeare's sonnets

I have tried lately to read Shakespeare, and found it so intolerably dull that it nauseated me.

Charles Darwin on William Shakespeare

A sycophant, a flatterer, a breaker of marriage vows, a whining and inconstant person.

Elizabeth Forsyth on William Shakespeare

Shakespeare never had six lines together without a fault. Perhaps you may find seven, but this does not refute my general assertion.

Samuel Johnson on William Shakespeare

The intensity of my impatience with him occasionally reaches such a pitch, that it would positively be a relief to me to dig him up and throw stones at him.

George Bernard Shaw on William Shakespeare, *Dramatic Opinions and Essays*

A strange, horrible business, but I suppose good enough for Shakespeare's day.

Queen Victoria giving her opinion of *King Lear*

The way Bernard Shaw believes in himself is very refreshing in these atheistic days when so many people believe in no God at all.

Israel Zangwill on George Bernard Shaw

He is an old bore; even the grave yawns for him.

Herbert Beerbohm Tree on Israel Zangwill

George too Shaw to be Good.

Dylan Thomas on George Bernard Shaw

He is the true Elizabethan blank-verse beast, itching to frighten other people with the superstitious terrors and cruelties in which he does not himself believe, and wallowing in blood, violence, muscularity of expression and strenuous animal passion as only literary men do when they become thoroughly depraved by solitary work, sedentary cowardice, and starvation of the sympathetic centres. It is not surprising to learn that Marlowe was stabbed in a tavern brawl: what would be utterly unbelievable would be his having succeeded in stabbing anyone else.

George Bernard Shaw on Christopher Marlowe, *Dramatic Opinions and Essays*

The first man to have cut a swathe through the theatre and left it strewn with virgins.

Frank Harris on George Bernard Shaw

He hasn't an enemy in the world, and none of his friends like him.

Oscar Wilde on George Bernard Shaw

He was over-dressed, pompous, snobbish, sentimental and vain. But he had an undeniable flair for the possibilities of commercial theatre.

Evelyn Waugh on Oscar Wilde

I really enjoy only his stage directions . . . He uses the English language like a truncheon.

Max Beerbohm on George Bernard Shaw

Mr Shaw is (I suspect) the only man on earth who has never written any poetry.

G. K. Chesterton on George Bernard Shaw

He writes like a Pakistani who has learned English when he was twelve years old in order to become a chartered accountant.
John Osborne on George Bernard Shaw in the *Manchester Guardian*

There are no human beings in Major Barbara; only animated points of view.
William Archer on *Major Barbara* by George Bernard Shaw, *World*

A good man fallen among Fabians.
Vladimir Ilich Lenin on George Bernard Shaw. Attrib.

An Irish smut dealer.
Anthony Comstock on George Bernard Shaw

A desiccated bourgeois ... a fossilized chauvinist, a self-satisfied Englishman.
Pravda on George Bernard Shaw, 1924

NORTHCLIFFE: The trouble with you, Shaw, is that you look as if there were a famine in the land.
SHAW: The trouble with you, Northcliffe, is that you look as if you were the cause of it.
George Bernard Shaw to Lord Northcliffe

I object to publishers: the one service they have done me is to teach me to do without them. They combine commercial rascality with artistic touchiness and pettiness, without being either good businessmen or fine judges of literature. All that is necessary in the production of a book is an author and a bookseller, without any intermediate parasite.
George Bernard Shaw

Great editors do not discover nor produce great authors; great authors create and produce great publishers.
John Farrar

When I split an infinitive, god damn it, I split it so it stays split.
Raymond Chandler, letter to his British publisher

A more horrible offence against Art than what you have put . . . on the cover of the Essays, has never been perpetrated even in Newcastle. I reject your handbill with disdain, with rage, with contumelious epithets . . . Of the hellish ugliness of the block of letterpress headed 'What the Press says', I cannot trust myself to write, lest I be betrayed into intemperance of language . . . Some time ago you mentioned something about changing the cover . . . This is to give you formal notice that if you do anything of the sort . . . I will have your heart's blood.
George Bernard Shaw, letter to his publisher

As repressed sadists are supposed to become policemen or butchers, so those with irrational fear of life become publishers.
Cyril Connolly

Nobody can read Freud without realizing he was the scientific equivalent of another nuisance, George Bernard Shaw.
Robert M. Hutchins on Sigmund Freud

He was meddling too much in my private life.
Tennessee Williams on why he had given up visiting his psychoanalyst

The trouble with Freud is that he never played the Glasgow Empire Saturday night.
Ken Dodd

Look, Nastase, we used to have a famous cricket match in this country called Gentlemen versus Players. The Gentlemen were put down on the scorecard as 'Mister' because they were gentlemen. By no stretch of the imagination can anybody call you a gentleman.

Trader Horn, Wimbledon umpire, on being asked to address Ilie Nastase as 'Mr Nastase'

A little mutant monstrosity that was born in the toxic dump of somebody's imagination.

The *Los Angeles Times* on Atlanta's 1996 Olympic mascot, Whatizit

You can't see as well as these fucking flowers – and they're fucking plastic.

John McEnroe to a line judge at the US Open, 1980

Advertising is the rattling of a stick inside a swill bucket.

George Orwell

People of the same trade seldom meet together but the conversation ends in a conspiracy against the public, or in some diversion to raise prices.

Adam Smith, *The Wealth of Nations*

If you would know what the Lord God thinks of money, you only have to look at those to whom He gives it.

Maurice Baring

Nothing links man to man like the frequent passage from hand to hand of cash.

Walter Richard Sickert

The salary of the chief executive of the large corporation is not a market award for achievement. It is frequently in the

nature of a warm personal gesture by the individual to himself.
John Kenneth Galbraith, *Annals of an Abiding Liberal*

Standing at the head of his troops, his drawn salary in his hand.
Henry Labouchère on the Duke of Clarence

The louder he talked of his honour the faster we counted our spoons.
Ralph Waldo Emerson, *The Conduct of Life*, 'Worship'

Finding a businessman interested in the arts is like finding chicken shit in the chicken salad.
Alice Neel

In studying the science of yesteryear one comes upon such interesting notions as gravity, electricity, and the roundness of the earth – while an examination of more recent phenomena shows a strong trend towards spray cheese, stretch denim, and the Moog synthesizer.
Fran Lebowitz

The first thing we do, let's kill all the lawyers.
William Shakespeare, *Henry VI, Part 2*

This is a British murder inquiry and some degree of justice must be seen to be more or less done.
Tom Stoppard, *Jumpers*

The majestic egalitarianism of the law, which forbids rich and poor alike to sleep under bridges, to beg in the streets, and to steal bread.
Anatole France, *The Red Lily*

The law-courts of England are open to all men, like the doors of the Ritz Hotel.
Charles, Lord Darling

I have come to regard the law-courts not as a cathedral but rather as a casino.
Richard Ingrams, in the *Guardian*

Laws are generally found to be nets of such a texture, as the little creep through, the great break through, and the middle-sized are alone entangled in.
William Shenstone

No brilliance is needed in the law. Nothing but common sense, and relatively clean fingernails.
John Mortimer, *A Voyage Round My Father*

I do not care to speak ill of any man behind his back, but I believe the gentleman is an *attorney*.
Samuel Johnson

A qadi [judge] who, when two parties part in peace,
Rekindles their dispute with binding words.
Indifferent to this world and its luxuries, he seems,
But in secret, he wouldn't say no to camel dung.

Oh, people, pause and hark
To the charming qualities of our qadi,
A homosexual, drunkard, fornicator, and takes bribes,
A tell-tale liar whose judgements follow his whims.
Ibn Ayas on Ibn al-Naqib, the Egyptian Chief Justice, Mameluke era (1250–1517)

My definition of utter waste is a coachload of lawyers going over a cliff, with three empty seats.

Lamar Hunt on the increasing problems of litigation in the National Football League

YOUNG BARRISTER: My lord, my unfortunate client . . . my lord, my unfortunate client . . . my lord, my . . . my . . .

LORD ELLENBOROUGH: Go on, sir, go on. As far as you have proceeded hitherto, the court is entirely in agreement with you.

Lord Ellenborough

Possibly not, m'Lud, but you are much better informed.

F. E. Smith to a judge who had failed to understand one of the barrister's lengthy legal speeches. The judge told Smith: 'I have listened to you, Mr Smith, but I am none the wiser.'

George Jeffreys pointed his stick at one of the rebels hauled before him in the famous 'bloody assizes', saying: 'There is a rogue at the end of my cane.'

'At which end, my Lord?' retorted the man.

Anonymous

It is not for me, m'Lud, to attempt to fathom the inscrutable workings of Providence.

F. E. Smith to Judge Willis after the judge had interrupted his lengthy discourse, asking, 'What do you suppose I am on the bench for, Mr Smith?'

LORD SANDWICH: You will die either on the gallows, or of the pox.

WILKES: That must depend on whether I embrace your lordship's principles or your mistress.

John Wilkes; sometimes attributed to Samuel Foote. Quoted in *Portrait of a Patriot* by Charles Chenevix-Trench

I have forgotten more law than you ever knew, but allow me to say, I have not forgotten much.

Judge John Maynard, replying to Judge Jeffreys's assertion that he was so old he had forgotten the law

CONVICTED CRIMINAL: As God is my judge – I am innocent.
JUDGE BIRKETT: He isn't; I am, and you're not!

Judge Norman Birkett

From every treetop some wild woods songster will carol his mating song, butterflies will sport in the sunshine, the busy bee will hum happy as it pursues its accustomed vocation. The gentle breeze will tease the tassels of the wild grasses, and all nature, Jose Manuel Miguel Xavier Gonzales, will be glad but you. You won't be here to enjoy it because I command the sheriff or some other officer of this county to lead you out to some remote spot, swing you by the neck from a knotting bough of a sturdy oak, and let you hang until you are dead.

And then, Jose Manuel Miguel Xavier Gonzales, I further command that such officer or officers retire quickly from your dangling corpse, that vultures may descend from the heavens upon your filthy body until nothing shall remain but bare, bleached bones of a cold-blooded, copper-colored, blood-thirsty, throat-cutting, chili-eating, sheep-herding, murdering son-of-a-bitch.

Transcript from US District Court, New Mexico Territory, 1881, in the case of *USA* v. *Gonzales*

There were only 27 Republicans in this town, and you have eaten four of them.
Nineteenth-century American judge, sentencing to death a convicted cannibal

Here comes counsel for the other side.
Sydney Smith on the arrival of the lawyer Lord Brougham at a performance of *The Messiah*

Prisoner, God has given you good abilities, instead of which you go about the country stealing ducks.
William Arabin, judge

Conscience is the inner voice that warns us somebody may be looking.
H. L. Mencken

We know of no spectacle so ridiculous as the British public in one of its periodical fits of morality.
Thomas Babington Macaulay

You see, I always divide people into two groups. Those who live by what they know to be a lie, and those who live by what they believe, falsely, to be the truth.
Christopher Hampton, *The Philanthropist*

Some men love truth so much that they seem to be in continual fear lest she should catch a cold on overexposure.
Samuel Butler

Self-interest speaks all sorts of tongues, and plays all sorts of roles, even that of disinterestedness.
François, Duc de La Rochefoucauld

An orgy looks particularly alluring seen through the mists of righteous indignation.
Malcolm Muggeridge

Dost thou think, because thou art virtuous, there shall be no more cakes and ale?
William Shakespeare, *Twelfth Night*

Religion is the venereal disease of mankind.
Henri de Montherlant

I shudder at the thought of religion, I flee the Bible as a viper, and revolt at the touch of a Christian, for their tender mercies may next fall upon my head.
G. J. Holyoake at a lecture in Cheltenham

Oysters are more beautiful than any religion ... There's nothing in Christianity or Buddhism that quite matches the sympathetic unselfishness of an oyster.
Andrei Dimitrievich Sakharov

Religion is the source of all imaginable follies and disturbances; it is the parent of fanaticism and civil discord; it is the enemy of mankind.
Voltaire

In your book you have used the word 'Flight' for the migration of the Holy Prophet from Mecca to Medina ... 'Hijrat' (migration) was a strategic withdrawal to a friendly place made according to plan, under Divine guidance. You will not like to use the word 'flight' when the British armies took to their heels at Dunkirk in World War II. How do you account for

using the word 'flight' for an event that has a religious sanctity
for the Muslim world?

Mr Irshad, a Muslim, to Bertrand Russell

September 16, 1963
Dear Mr Irshad,
    Thank you for your letter. 1. The British armies did flee
from Dunkirk just as Mohammed fled from Mecca to Medina.
2. I do not believe that Mohammed or anyone else was
impelled by 'divine inspiration'. 3. To call flight 'strategic
withdrawal' is ludicrous. 4. The picture of the prophet should
be displayed as a matter of interest to students and scholars. 5.
Chauvinism is harmful and also accompanies the absence of
any humour or humility.
Yours sincerely
BERTRAND RUSSELL
P.S. I am opposed to all superstition: Muslim, Christian, Jewish
or Buddhist.

Bertrand Russell, replying to Mr Irshad

Religion is the sign of the oppressed creature, the feeling of a
heartless world and the spirit of conditions which are unspiri-
tual. It is the opium of the people.

Karl Marx

Many people think they have religion when they are troubled
with dyspepsia.

Robert G. Ingersoll, *Liberty of Man, Woman and Child*

Many people believe that they are attracted by God, or by
Nature, when they are only repelled by man.

William Ralph Inge, *More Lay Thoughts of a Dean*

As you, Sir, have introduced religion into this meeting, which I have carefully avoided in my lecture, I will answer your question frankly and sincerely ... Home colonization is an economic scheme, and as we can ill bear the burden of God here, he may lie rather heavy on our hands there. Our national debt and our national taxes hang like millstones round the neck of the poor man's prosperity, saying nothing of the enormous gatherings of capitalists in addition to all this; and in the face of our misery and want we are charged twenty millions more for the worship of God ... I appeal to your heads and your pockets if we are not too poor to have a God. If poor men cost the state so much, they would be put like officers on half-pay. I think that while our distress lasts it would be wise to do the same thing with the Deity.

G. J. Holyoake at a lecture in Cheltenham, 1842, on home colonization, when asked by a clergyman in the audience what provision should be made for God in the new colonies. For these statements Holyoake was prosecuted for blasphemy and sentenced to six months imprisonment, during which time his daughter died of starvation.

The whole religious complexion of the modern world is due to the absence from Jerusalem of a lunatic asylum.

Havelock Ellis

Heaven, as conventionally conceived, is a place so inane, so dull, so useless, so miserable, that nobody has ever ventured to describe a whole day in heaven, though plenty of people have described a day at the seaside.

George Bernard Shaw

Probably no invention came more easily to man than Heaven.

Georg Christoph Lichtenberg, *Aphorisms*

There is a very good saying that if triangles invented a god, they would make him three-sided.

Baron de Montesquieu, *Lettres persanes*

An honest God is the noblest work of man.

Robert G. Ingersoll, *The Gods*

God can stand being told by Professor Ayer and Marghanita Laski that He doesn't exist.

J. B. Priestley, in the *Listener*

Man is quite insane. He wouldn't know how to create a maggot and he creates Gods by the dozen.

Michel de Montaigne, *Essais*

God is the immemorial refuge of the incompetent, the helpless, the miserable. They find not only sanctuary in His arms, but also a kind of superiority, soothing to their macerated egos; He will set them above their betters.

H. L. Mencken

An inordinate fondness for beetles.

J. B. S. Haldane, when asked what inferences could be drawn about the nature of God from a study of his works

If God were suddenly condemned to live the life which He has inflicted on men, He would kill Himself.

Alexandre Dumas fils, *Pensées d'album*

Forgive, O Lord, my little jokes on Thee
And I'll forgive Thy great big one on me.

Robert Frost

[God] invented the giraffe, the elephant, and the cat. He has no real style, He just goes on trying other things.
Pablo Picasso

Her conception of God was certainly not orthodox. She felt towards Him as she might have felt towards a glorified sanitary engineer; and in some of her speculations she seems hardly to distinguish between the Deity and the Drains.
Lytton Strachey on Florence Nightingale

My dear child, you must believe in God in spite of what the clergy tell you.
Benjamin Jowett, theologian and classicist, quoted in Margot Asquith's *Autobiography*

I asserted – and I repeat – that a man has no reason to be ashamed of having an ape for his grandfather. If there were an ancestor whom I should feel shame in recalling it would rather be a *man* – a man of restless and versatile intellect – who, not content with an equivocal success in his own sphere of activity, plunges into scientific questions with which he has no real acquaintance, only to obscure them by an aimless rhetoric, and distract the attention of his hearers from the real point at issue by eloquent digressions and skilled appeal to religious prejudice.
T. H. Huxley, biologist, replying to Bishop Wilberforce in an Oxford debate on Darwin's theory of evolution

Operationally, God is beginning to resemble not a ruler but the last fading smile of a Cheshire cat.
Julian Huxley, biologist and first director-general of UNESCO, *Religion without Revelation*

. . . the sort of atheist who does not so much disbelieve God as personally dislike Him.
George Orwell, *Down and Out in Paris and London*

I have no need of that hypothesis.
Pierre-Simon, Marquis de Laplace, on being asked by Napoleon why he had not mentioned God in his book on the universe

For a priest to turn a man when he lies a–dying, is just like one that has a long time solicited a woman, and cannot obtain his end; at length makes her drunk, and so lies with her.
John Selden

Every day people are straying away from the church and going back to God. Really.
Lenny Bruce

While I cannot be regarded as a pillar, I must be regarded as a buttress of the church, because I support it from the outside.
Lord Melbourne. Attrib.

It is hard to tell where MCC ends and the Church of England begins.
J. B. Priestley, in the *New Statesman*

He had tried the knightly way and failed, ignominiously. In his misery he turned to religion, and there, in religion, discovered a new field for achieving the personal distinction for which his soul so ardently and incessantly longed. The world refused to recognize him as Assisi's greatest soldier. Very well. It should recognize him as Assisi's greatest man of God.
Aldous Huxley on St Francis of Assisi

The numerous vermin of mendicant friars, Franciscans, Dominicans, Augustins, Carmelites, who swarmed in this century [the thirteenth], with habits and institutions variously ridiculous, disgraced religion, learning, and common sense. They seized on scholastic philosophy as a science particularly suited to their minds; and, excepting only Friar Bacon, they all preferred words to things. The subtle, the profound, the irrefragable, the angelic, and the seraphic Doctor acquired those pompous titles by filling ponderous volumes with a small number of technical terms, and a much smaller number of ideas. Universities arose in every part of Europe, and thousands of students employed their lives upon these grave follies.

Edward Gibbon on medieval Christendom

With this I am at the end and I pronounce my judgement. I *condemn* Christianity. I raise against the Christian church the most terrible of all accusations that any accuser ever uttered. It is to me the highest of all conceivable corruptions. It has had the will to the last corruption that is even possible. The Christian church has left nothing untouched by its corruption; it has turned every value into an un-value, every truth into a lie, every integrity into a vileness of the soul. Let anyone dare to speak to me of its 'humanitarian' blessings! To *abolish* any distress ran counter to its deepest advantages: it lived on distress, it *created* distress to eternalize *itself*.

The worm of sin, for example: with this distress the church first enriched mankind. The 'equality of all souls before God', this falsehood, this *pretext* for the rancour of all the base-minded, this explosive of a concept which eventually became a revolution, modern idea, and the principle of decline of the whole order of society – is *Christian* dynamite. 'Humanitarian' blessings of Christianity! To breed out of *humanitas* a self-contradiction, an art of self-violation, a will to lie at any price, a repugnance, a contempt for all good and honest instincts! Those are some of the blessings of Christianity!

Parasitism is the *only* practice of the church; with its ideal of anaemia, its 'holiness', draining all blood, all love, all hope for life; the beyond as the will to negate every reality; the cross as the mark of recognition for the most subterranean conspiracy that ever existed – against health, beauty, whatever has turned out well, courage, spirit, *graciousness* of the soul, *against life itself*.

This eternal indictment of Christianity I will write on all walls, wherever there are walls – I have letters to make even the blind see.

I call Christianity the one great curse, the one great innermost corruption, the one great instinct of revenge, for which no means is poisonous, stealthy, subterranean, *small* enough – I call it the one immortal blemish of mankind.

Friedrich Nietzsche, *The Antichrist*

I have to believe in the Apostolic Succession. There is no other way of explaining the descent of the Bishop of Exeter from Judas Iscariot.

Sydney Smith

The Christian religion not only was at first attended with miracles, but even at this day cannot be believed by any reasonable person without one.

David Hume, *Essays*, 'Of Miracles'

I am a Catholic. As far as possible I go to Mass every day. As far as possible I kneel down and tell these beads every day. If you reject me on account of my religion, I shall thank God that he has spared me the indignity of being your representative.

Hilaire Belloc, MP for Salford (1906–10), in his first election campaign

Bad weather is God's way of telling us to burn more Catholics.

Rowan Atkinson, *Blackadder*

We know these new English Catholics. They are the last word in Protest. They are Protestants protesting against Protestantism.

D. H. Lawrence, letter to Lady Cynthia Asquith

I don't feel the attraction of the Kennedys at all ... I don't think they are Christians; they may be Catholics but they are not Christians.

Mary McCarthy

A single friar who goes counter to all Christianity for a thousand years must be wrong.

Charles V, Holy Roman Emperor, on Martin Luther, at the Diet of Worms

A Lutheran's foot has six toes.

Polish insult

Puritanism – The haunting fear that someone, somewhere, may be happy.

H. L. Mencken

Mencken, with his filthy verbal haemorrhages, is so low down in the moral scale, so damnable dirty, so vile and degenerate, that when his time comes to die it will take a special dispensation from Heaven to get him into the bottommost pit of Hell.

Letter to H. L. Mencken, in the *Jackson News*

Faith may be defined briefly as an illogical belief in the occurrence of the improbable.

H. L. Mencken

Mr Mencken did not degenerate from an ape, but an ass. And in the process of 'evolution' the tail was eliminated, the ears became shorter, and the hind parts smaller; but the ability to bray was increased, intensified, amplified, and otherwise assified about one million times.

J. D. Tedder on H. L. Mencken

The chief contribution of Protestantism to human thought is its massive proof that God is a bore.

H. L. Mencken

The Puritan hated bear-baiting, not because it gave pain to the bear, but because it gave pleasure to the spectators.

Thomas Babington Macaulay, *History of England*

Sir, the pretending of extraordinary revelations and gifts of the Holy Ghost is an horrid thing, a very horrid thing.

Bishop Joseph Butler to one of the Wesleys, quoted in Wesley, *Works*, XIII

No visit to Dove Cottage, Grasmere, is complete without examining the outhouse where Hazlitt's father, a Unitarian minister of strong liberal views, attempted to put his hand up Dorothy Wordsworth's skirt.

Alan Coren

A base impudent brazen-faced villain, a spiteful ignorant pedant, a gross idolater, a great liar, a mere slanderer, an evil man, hardened against all shame [while his book is] full of insolence and abuse, chicanery and nonsense, detestable, misty, erroneous, wicked, vile, pernicious, terrible, and horrid doctrines, tending to corrupt the mind and stupefy the conscience, with gross iniquity, audacious hostility, pitiful evasion, base, palpable, shocking, and solemn deceit, clouds of gross, abominable, and absolute falsehoods, foul, artful, base, with wicked and horrid reproaches, malicious invectives, low quibbles, unmeaning puffs, unbounded rancour, scurrilous, gross, and virulent abuse, monstrous, stupid, and intolerable absurdity, poor and palpable sophistry, idiotical construction, blasphemous comparisons, foppish insolence, senseless jargon, the style of a bully, rude imputations, profane banter and burlesque, perfect downright barefaced and impudent forgery, abusive rage, base dealing, violent and shameful opposition, high and poetical rant, solemn juggling with God and man, chimerical notions, virulent invective, mock sorrow, nauseous repetition, horrid extravagance, treacherous disingenuity, scurrilous reason, base intendment, injurious dealing, [and finally] dreadful language.

Revd Adam Gibb, anti-Burgher leader, ed. Tertius Gaudens, reviewing a pamphlet by the Burgher minister, the Revd Archibald Hill, 1782. Quoted in *Scottish Pageant 1707–1802*, ed. Agnes Mure Mackenzie

No kingdom has ever had as many civil wars as the kingdom of Christ.

Baron de Montesquieu, *Lettres persanes*

HECKLER: Christianity has been on the earth for 2,000 years, and look at the state of the world today.
SOPER: Water has been on the earth longer than that, and look at the colour of your neck.

Donald Soper

It was just one of those parties which got out of hand.

Lenny Bruce on the Crucifixion

If Jesus Christ were to come today, people would not even crucify him. They would ask him to dinner, and hear what he had to say, and make fun of it.

Thomas Carlyle

Things have come to a pretty pass when religion is allowed to invade the sphere of private life.

Lord Melbourne. Attrib.

Damn it all, another bishop dead. I verily believe they die to vex me.

Lord Melbourne. Attrib.

There can hardly be a town in the South of England where you could throw a brick without hitting the niece of a bishop.

George Orwell, *The Road to Wigan Pier*

CLERGYMAN: How did you like my sermon, Mr Canning?
CANNING: You were brief.
CLERGYMAN: Yes, you know I avoid being tedious.

CANNING: But you were tedious.
George Canning

Yes, about ten minutes.
Duke of Wellington after a vicar asked him whether there was anything he
would like his sermon to be about

A clergyman has nothing to do but to be slovenly and selfish –
read the newspaper, watch the weather, and quarrel with his
wife. His curate does all the work and the business of his own
life is to dine.
Jane Austen, *Mansfield Park*

Parson,
   I have, during my life, detested many men; but never any
one so much as you ... Priests have, in all ages, been remarkable for cool and deliberate and unrelenting cruelty; but it
seems to be reserved for the Church of England to produce
one who has a just claim to the atrocious pre-eminence. No
assemblage of words can give an appropriate designation of
you; and therefore, as being the single word which best suits
the character of such a man, I call you Parson ...
William Cobbett to Thomas Malthus

When the white man came we had the land and they had the
Bibles; now they have the land and we have the Bibles.
Dan George, Canadian Indian chief, who acted in a number of films,
including *Little Big Man*

Whenever we read the obscene stories, the voluptuous
debaucheries, the cruel and torturous executions, the unrelenting vindictiveness, with which more than half the Bible is

filled, it would be more consistent that we called it the word of a demon than the Word of God. It is a history of wickedness, that has served to corrupt and brutalize mankind; and for my own part, I sincerely detest it, as I detest everything that is cruel...

As to the Christian system of faith, it appears to me as a species of atheism — a sort of religious denial of God. It professes to believe in a man rather than in God. It is as near to atheism as twilight is to darkness. It introduces between man and his Maker an opaque body, which it calls a Redeemer, as the moon introduces her opaque self between the earth and the sun, and it produces by this means a religious or irreligious eclipse of the light. It has put the whole orbit of reason into shade.

Tom Paine, *The Age of Reason*

That revolting odious Jew production, called Bible, has been for ages the idol of all sorts of blockheads, the glory of knaves, and the disgust of wise men. It is a history of lust, sodomies, wholesale slaughtering, and horrible depravity, that the vilest parts of all other histories, collected into one book, could not parallel. Priests tell us that this concentration of abominations was written by a god; all the world believe priests, or they would rather have thought it the outpourings of some devil.

Charles Southwell in the *Oracle of Reason*, an openly atheistic weekly newspaper, 1841. Southwell was fined £100 and imprisoned for a year.

Jesus was a crackpot.

Bhagwan Shree Rajneesh

It is so stupid of modern civilization to have given up believing in the devil when he is the only explanation of it.

Ronald Knox, Catholic priest and writer, *Let Dons Delight*

A liar and a father of lies.

Dante on the Devil, *Inferno*, XXIII

Even in the valley of the shadow of death, two and two do not make six.

Leo Tolstoy on his deathbed, refusing to reconcile himself with the Russian Orthodox Church

Index

Index

Index

Index

Index

Index

Index